SYNAGOGUES

SYNAGOGUES

SAMUEL D. GRUBER

MetroBooks

MetroBooks

An Imprint of Friedman/Fairfax Publishers

Library of Congress Cataloging-in-Publication Data available upon request.

ISBN 1-56799-742-2

Editor: Celeste Sollod
Art Director: Jeff Batzli
Designer: Howard P. Johnson, Communigrafix, Inc.
Photography Editor: Wendy Missan
Production Director: Karen Matsu Greenberg

Color separations by ColourScan
Printed in Hong Kong by Midas Printing Limited

10 9 8 7 6 5 4 3 2 1

For bulk purchases and special sales, please contact:
Friedman/Fairfax Publishers
Attention: Sales Department
15 West 26th Street
New York, NY 10010
212/685-6610   FAX 212/685-1307

Visit our website:
http://www.metrobooks.com

To my parents,
Shirley Moskowitz Gruber and Jacob W. Gruber

ACKNOWLEDGMENTS

PRIMARY THANKS GO TO the World Monuments Fund, which, through the establishment of its Jewish Heritage Program, has allowed me to visit and learn about many of the places described in this book. WMF President Bonnie Burnham and JHP Chairman Hon. Ronald S. Lauder have always been encouraging and supportive of my work.

M. Raina and Philipp Fehl, founders of the International Survey of Jewish Monuments, first sparked my interest in historic synagogues, and Alan Berger was the first to invite me to give a university course on the architecture of the synagogue. As a result, special thanks go to my students at Syracuse University, Cornell University, and Binghamton University, who have patiently heard much of this material and shown me where explanation is needed.

My thanks to David Sassoon, who helped shape the introductory chapter. I cannot mention here everyone who has shared knowledge and experience with me, but special thanks go to a number of researchers who have, over the years, introduced me to the bounty of synagogue design—Carol Herselle Krinsky and Maria and Kazimierz Piechotka have always been generous mentors, and Eleonora Bergman, Marilyn Chiat, Ruth Ellen Gruber, Thomas Hubka, Dominique Jarrasse, Sharman Kadish, David Kaufman, Elias Messinas, Nicholas Stavroulakis, and Joel Zack are all colleagues and collaborators who have taught me much about the synagogues of the world. Robert Lyons and Isaiah Wyner first exposed me to the wonders of synagogues in Arab lands through their marvelous photographs of Morocco and Syria.

Finally, I wish to thank my wife, Judith Meighan, for her companionship and support of my work, and her loving patience when I have traveled and she has not.

CONTENTS

THE NATURE OF SYNAGOGUES

SINCE THE DESTRUCTION OF THE Second Temple in 70 C.E., the synagogue has been the center of Jewish communal life and worship. A synagogue (from the Greek word *synagein*, "to bring together") requires only an enclosed space to allow a congregation to assemble for prayer and to hear the Torah (Five Books of Moses) read. Synagogues can also serve secular purposes, used frequently for community assemblies and legal proceedings.

Although for Jews synagogues remain, in the prophet Ezekiel's words, as "lesser sanctuaries," nonetheless in the post-Temple period Jews have lavished attention on synagogues when there was the opportunity to do so. In the Diaspora (the lands outside Israel), the multipurpose synagogue came to represent Jewish life and symbolize community identity. It also became, until recently, the focus of Jewish artistic endeavors. Beginning in the nineteenth century, many synagogues came to be called "temples," reflecting

how in the minds of many the synagogue has truly become the spiritual home of Judaism.

Architectural historian Carol Herselle Krinsky has written how synagogues "reveal especially clearly the connections between architecture and society." The choices made in the building of synagogues can tell us much about the realities and aspirations of Jewish communities at different times and in different places, or of distinct Jewish congregations coexisting at the same time and place.

The basic functions of the synagogue had been defined by the first century B.C.E. and these have remained essentially unchanged throughout the centuries. But it was not until the period following

the destruction of the Second Temple that synagogues took on their central role in Jewish societies. Primarily a house of prayer, the synagogue was often offered to the community as a classroom for children and adults as well. It could also serve as a temporary repository of funds. Caches of coins have been found beneath the floors of several excavated synagogues.

In the Jewish communities reestablished throughout Judea and the Galilee under Roman rule in the centuries following the destruction of the Temple and the dispersion of the Jewish population, synagogues became major urban monuments–the visual focus of Jewish town life and identity—and so they have continued until today.

Opposite: THE TEMPLE IN DEJ, ROMANIA, BUILT IN 1907, IS TYPICAL OF THE LARGE SYNAGOGUES BUILT IN THE AUSTRO-HUNGARIAN EMPIRE AT THE TURN OF THE CENTURY. THE DECALOGUE (THE REPRESENTATION OF THE TABLETS OF LAW GIVEN TO MOSES ON MOUNT SINAI), SET AT THE SYNAGOGUE'S HIGHEST POINT, ANNOUNCES ITS JEWISH IDENTITY.

In seventeenth-century Amsterdam, Daniel Levi de Barrious celebrated the consecration of the new Portuguese Synagogue (1675) with the following poem:

> *The mists dissolved when the old desire*
> *for the holy law awoke in the people who so ardently*
> *worship the great God, and their glorious temple*
> *arose in this prosperous city.*
> *Sing its praises on high, tell of its*
> *beauty near and far. It is a ladder*
> *for the angels to this earth, and for Israel*
> *a gateway to heaven.*

FORM AND FUNCTION

What Makes A Synagogue?

Tൟ

THERE IS NO SINGLE SYNAGOGUE TYPE and not all synagogues are architecturally distinctive. Indeed, many Jewish congregations, especially when they are new and poor, have merely adapted preexisting spaces with little change for their religious purposes. Synagogues often resemble churches or mosques in layout and articulation, but there are certain essential features that every synagogue must have for religious practices, and many features that are expected due to tradition.

THE ARK AND THE BIMAH

FIRST AND FOREMOST, the ark (*Aron ha-Kodesh;* or *hechal* in the Sephardic tradition, the Jewish culture that flourished in medieval Spain), the cabinet that holds the Torah scrolls, and the *bimah* (*tevah* in Sephardic tradition; pl. *bimot*), the platform where the leader of the service stands and from which the Torah is read, are constant in all synagogues, no matter when and where they are built, and what decorative style they adopt.

The Torah scroll, which contains the words of God, is the holiest object in Jewish life. The ark and bimah, because they are essential to the reading of the Torah, and because they come in regular contact with the scroll, are the holiest parts of a synagogue. It is not surprising, then, that in synagogue architecture the designs of the ark and the bimah have been given the greatest attention.

The physical relationship between ark and bimah reflects their roles in the Jewish service and creates a strong dynamic. There is a visual link, reinforced during services by the processional of the Torah, which is carried from ark to bimah and then back again, to the accompaniment of the congregation singing.

Three basic arrangements of ark and bimah dominate. In the Sephardic tradition, hechal and tevah are often placed at opposite ends of the room, and the congregation sits facing the axis between them. Congregants turn their heads from one to the other, as if the two furnishings were in dialogue. However, in traditional Ashkenazic (referring to German and eastern European Jews) synagogues, such as the central-plan wooden synagogues in Poland, the centrally placed bimah creates a different dynamic, where the congregation encircles the

Pages 10-11: THE ISAAC M. WISE SYNAGOGUE IN CINCINNATI, OHIO, KNOWN AS THE PLUM STREET SYNAGOGUE, WAS, WHEN BUILT, THE FULLEST EXPRESSION OF AMERICAN REFORM PRACTICE. HERE, IN A CHURCHLIKE SETTING, THE BIMAH AND ARK WERE COMBINED IN FRONT OF THE EAST WALL. THE RICHLY DECORATED ARK, WHICH IS THE PRIMARY FOCUS IN THE BUILDING, IS FLANKED BY MENORAHS. HANGING ABOVE IT IS THE *NER TAMID* (ETERNAL LIGHT), AND SET IN A HIGH WINDOW IS A DECALOGUE. *Page 11, detail:* TORAH SCROLLS REST IN THEIR CASES, KNOWN AS *TIKS*, IN THE HECHAL AT THE RACQY SYNAGOGUE IN DAMASCUS. *Above:* ONE OF THE FEW SYNAGOGUES IN AUSTRIA TO SURVIVE THE HOLOCAUST IS THE PRIVATE SYNAGOGUE OF COURT JEW (A PROMINENT JEW WITH CLOSE CONNECTIONS TO THE ROYAL COURT) AND CHIEF RABBI OF HUNGARY SAMSON WERTHEIMER (1658–1724), AT EISENSTADT, NOW A MUSEUM. IT IS THE ONLY SURVIVING PRIVATE SYNAGOGUE IN EUROPE. THE ELEGANT ARK IS FLANKED BY TWO PAIRS OF IONIC COLUMNS, TYPICAL OF THE SYNAGOGUE'S EIGHTEENTH-CENTURY CLASSICAL ARCHITECTURE. *Opposite:* THE ARK OF THE SYNAGOGUE AT APOSTAG, HUNGARY, BUILT IN 1822, REPEATS MANY OF THE SAME MOTIFS OF EISENSTADT. TYPICALLY, THE ARK IS INTRODUCED BY THREE STEPS, WHICH A CONGREGANT MUST ASCEND. THE SYNAGOGUE, LOCATED IN A FARMING VILLAGE, WAS RESTORED IN 1988 AS THE TOWN LIBRARY.

reader. Lastly, in modern times, Conservative and Reform Jews have moved the bimah to the front of the congregation immediately before the ark. The result is a more hierarchical arrangement, exactly what the "decorum"-seeking Jews of nineteenth-century European and American cities who began the Reform and Conservative movements wanted.

Very early on it became accepted practice to place the ark against the wall of the synagogue that faces Jerusalem and to have the door to the prayer hall opposite the ark. Though seating arrangements vary, it is usual for worshipers to face the ark (and hence Jerusalem) while praying. The ark can be made of any material, and can be any size or shape, but generally it is rectangular in form. In early synagogues, the Torah scrolls were kept in movable chests, which may also have served as readers' tables.

In some early synagogues, apses or other architectural devices focused attention on the ark placement. By the Middle Ages, the ark had become a vertical but still freestanding cabinet, often quite ornate. From the sixteenth-century on, the practice of building the ark directly into the synagogue wall and elevated above the main floor of the sanctuary, and approached by steps, became common, especially in the masonry synagogues of central Europe.

The bimah can be a simple table, but it is usually more elaborate. The bimah platform may even be covered by a canopy, and coverings of ironwork, as in Cracow, Poland; gilt metal, in Fez, Morocco; masonry, in Lancut, Poland; and wood, in Damascus, Syria, have all been used.

INTERIOR PLANS

INTERIOR PLANS for synagogues take many forms. The basilica plan, featuring a wide central aisle and narrower side aisles often terminating in a projecting apse, which was inherited from Roman architecture and used for Christian churches, was popular in early synagogue construction. Multi-aisle synagogues were common in antiquity and in medieval Spain.

The hall plan, which is simply an open, usually rectangular, room with no columnar obstructions was often preferred, especially for smaller congregations. Hall plans were of more modest dimensions because of the limitations of roof spans. Private synagogues, often within or attached to a patron's house, usually took this form. The HaLevi Synagogue in Toledo, Spain, is an example of a lavish hall plan.

The interior spaces of hall-plan synagogues were often exceptionally tall in relation to their width. Galleries, usually reserved for women, were sometimes inserted above the main floor,

attached to two or three sides of the room. This setup maximized the seating potential of the space and created a theaterlike atmosphere, which was often heightened by rich decoration.

In medieval Germany and other parts of central Europe a double-nave plan (which can still be seen in Worms, Prague, and Cracow), consisting of a vaulted space divided into two equal aisles by a central row of columns or piers, was frequently adopted. This had the advantage of being perceived as quite distinct from a church, but it was inadequate because it obstructed sight lines to the ark, which was on the same axis as the supporting columns. To minimize this problem, the entrances to these synagogues were located at oblique angles to the ark, and benches were set around the periphery of the space, allowing broad sight lines.

The use of lighter wood and of improved masonry vaulting after the sixteenth century allowed the development of broader, loftier interiors. In Poland, a new vaulted hall type, often based on the ark and bimah central plan, worked well for centuries and helped create some of the most magnificent synagogue interiors. The wide-open space and the high ceilings also encouraged the development of increasingly ornate bimot, which often copied in smaller form the plan of the synagogue. Tragically, most of these spaces, often the highest expression of this type of design, were destroyed during World War II.

In the nineteenth century, a new form of synagogue interior articulation that followed much more closely upon the lines of traditional church architecture was developed. Reform Jews adopted more "propriety" in the worship

THE YOCHANAN BEN ZAKKAI SYNAGOGUE IN JERUSALEM WAS ERECTED BY THE CITY'S SEPHARDIC COMMUNITY IN THE LATE SIXTEENTH CENTURY. THE TEVAH IS CENTRALLY PLACED DIRECTLY OPPOSITE THE ARK.

Opposite: The Fabric Synagogue (also known as the Great Synagogue) in Timisoara, Romania, was designed by celebrated synagogue architect Lipot Baumhorn and built in 1899. One of three synagogues in the city, and one of the grandest synagogues in all of Romania, it is an imposing central plan building with a large dome and corner turrets. Inside is a rich and very eclectic mix of decorative forms. *Above:* The restored eighteenth-century synagogue at Tykocin, Poland, is noteworthy for its large four-pillared bimah and ornate rococo ark. Both are made of masonry covered with painted plaster, which accounts for their partial survival. The walls of the synagogues were covered with Hebrew prayer texts.

service, with less spontaneous prayer and more united response.

The bimah was moved from the center of the space and positioned adjacent to or immediately in front of the ark. A single set of steps led to the enlarged platform, and all ritual and reading were centralized in this single location. Pulpits were also added, since preaching and sermons by rabbis, often in the vernacular language or in German, now became an important part of the public service. This was not entirely new. Some older synagogues also had this arrangement, but never to the scale developed in the nineteenth century.

DECORATION

SYNAGOGUES HAVE always been decorated. The Spanish-Jewish scholar Profiat Duran wrote in the fourteenth century that looking at beautiful shapes enlarged and enlivened the heart.

The ruins of the synagogue of Pinczow, in Poland, make it clear that the walls were painted in decorative motifs or with the texts of prayers. In other Polish synagogues in Tykocin and Lancut, decorations have been restored. Yet other synagogues, especially in Spain and North Africa, were covered with ornate panel-

ing or tiling. Often, especially in Italy, rare woods or gilding was used.

The level of ostentatious decoration in the nineteenth century was, however, unparalleled, if only because of the enormous size of the structures erected. The freedom and wealth of the communities also contributed, as did the taste of the era. The Oranienburgerstrasse Synagogue in Berlin, the Dohany Street Synagogue in Budapest, and hundreds of other slightly smaller structures throughout Europe, America, and Australia testify to the confidence and exuberance of nineteenth-century Jewry.

Women's Areas

Seating can be arranged in many ways, though in Orthodox synagogues separate seating is required for women. This is often provided in a gallery, but a barrier (mechitzah) can also be used in smaller spaces to divide women's and men's sections. Medieval synagogues often featured separate women's rooms, usually in annexes connected to the main space with small windows or grates. In Carpentras, France, women were relegated to a basement room beneath the sanctuary, connected only by a floor grill to the activity above.

In later versions of the hall plan, raised galleries, supported by columns or piers, wrapped around three sides of the space to serve female congregants. This form of synagogue, always popular in urban areas because it allowed maximum seating within limited space, was particularly prevalent in the United States until recently.

THIS ORTHODOX SYNAGOGUE IN PRESOV, SLOVAKIA, BUILT IN 1893, MIXES CLASSICAL AND MOORISH DECORATIVE ELEMENTS IN A TRADITIONAL BASILICA PLAN. THE BIMAH, FROM WHERE THE TORAH IS READ TO THE CONGREGATION, IS NEAR THE CENTER OF THE BUILDING. IRON COLUMNS SUPPORT THE GALLERIES, WHICH WERE RESERVED FOR WOMEN. THIS VIEW SHOWS THE GALLERY CEILING DECORATED WITH A SIX-POINTED STAR: THE "SHIELD OF DAVID" OR "STAR OF DAVID." THIS SYMBOL, NOW WIDELY UNDERSTOOD AS A POSITIVE SYMBOL OF JUDAISM, WAS ONLY OCCASIONALLY USED IN THE NINETEENTH CENTURY, THUS ITS PLACEMENT IN THIS SYNAGOGUE IN A RATHER OUT-OF-THE-WAY SPOT.

Opposite: The Orthodox synagogue of Miskolc, Hungary, was built from 1856 to 1863, based on designs by Ludwig Forster. The wide, tall-galleried nave ends in an impressive ark surmounted by a Decalogue. Note the window in the east wall behind the ark, with tracery in a pattern of six-pointed stars. *Above:* Ludwig Forster also designed the Leopoldstrasse (Templegasse) Synagogue in Vienna and the Dohany Street Synagogue in Budapest—the two capitals of the Austro-Hungarian Empire. Forster was a pioneer in introducing exotic Moorish designs into synagogues—clearly evident in this dome from the Dohany Street Synagogue, the largest synagogue in Europe, which was fully restored in the 1990s.

IN THE BEGINNING

The Synagogue in the Ancient World

EVIDENCE INDICATES THAT SYNAGOGUES existed in Egypt by the third century B.C.E., but we know nothing of the appearance of these buildings, or what exactly took place within them. In the Holy Land, synagogues existed before the destruction of the Second Temple, but these appear not to have played a central organizing role within Jewish life. They served a variety of social and religious purposes, supplementing but not replacing visitation to the Temple and participation in Temple ritual.

SYNAGOGUES IN ROMAN TIMES

JEWISH COMMUNITIES were established throughout the Roman Empire, and each community presumably had a synagogue, though these could have been no more than rooms in houses, similar to the earliest Christian churches. At least thirteen synagogues were situated within Rome itself.

The Jewish historian Josephus, in his description of the Jewish revolt against Roman rule (67–70 C.E.), mentions synagogues serving as meeting halls where communities gathered to discuss the danger posed toward them and to plan their tactics. In the first century C.E., Saint Paul preached in the synagogues of Damascus, Salamis (Cyprus), Antioch of Pisidia, Iconium, Thessalonica, Berea, Corinth, and Ephesus. Archaeological finds have revealed remains of many ancient synagogues, and while most are located in the Middle East, there are some from Stobi (Yugoslavia); Ostia and Bova Marina in Italy; and Hamman Lif in Tunisia.

A few synagogues from cities and strongholds destroyed by the Romans are known. The best and most securely identified example is from Gamla, in Northern Israel, where an almost square space was surrounded by three levels of built-in benches on each side. Congregants faced the central open space, where the ark was presumably displayed and a table was erected for reading the Torah scrolls. The main hall had four columns to support the roof. Synagogues such as this one probably served a variety of purposes.

Synagogue architecture owed much to local building traditions and the prevalent architectural styles. It is natural for buildings of a minority to reflect the cultural features of the

Pages 22-23: THE CENTRAL DOORWAY AND COLUMNS OF THE ANCIENT SYNAGOGUE OF BAR'AM, ISRAEL, SITUATED IN THE NORTHERN GALILEE, ARE TYPICAL OF THE RICHLY CARVED SYNAGOGUES IN THE REGION, WHICH DATE TO THE ROMAN PERIOD. *Page 23, detail:* MENORAHS, RECALLING THOSE USED IN THE TEMPLE, HAVE BEEN PART OF SYNAGOGUE DECORATION SINCE ANCIENT TIMES. *Above:* SOLOMON'S TEMPLE, BELIEVED TO HAVE BEEN BUILT IN THE TENTH CENTURY B.C.E., WAS DESTROYED IN 586 B.C.E. THE TEMPLE WAS REBUILT BY KING HEROD BETWEEN 39 AND 4 B.C.E., THEN DESTROYED AGAIN IN 70 C.E. THIS MODEL OF THE TEMPLE IS BASED ON DESCRIPTIONS, DEPICTIONS ON COINS, AND ARCHAEOLOGICAL EXCAVATION. HEROD'S DESIGN JOINED ANCIENT NEAR EASTERN MASSING WITH GRECO-ROMAN DETAILING, AS SEEN IN THE COMBINATION OF THE RICHLY DECORATED ROOF AND THE TALL CORINTHIAN COLUMNS FLANKING THE ENTRANCE.

majority, and the art and architecture of the synagogue displays a conflicting relationship with dominant Classical forms. The style of building or representation is often clearly Roman. The organization of space in buildings, however, and the content of decoration reveal specific Jewish cultural or liturgical adaptations.

All the buildings were rectilinear, usually with plain exteriors, though some had decorated door lintels displaying Jewish symbols, most commonly the menorah. Construction was quite good, and impressive masonry walls of some early Galilee synagogues employ cut stones blocks ten feet (3m) long. During the Byzantine period, from the fourth century on, synagogue exteriors became plainer. Whether this was a reaction to anti-Jewish policies, which were increasingly enacted (if not always enforced), or simply a stylistic shift is unclear. Certainly, in both Jewish and Christian architecture there is more emphasis on the building interiors (where congregations actually gathered together) than their exteriors.

Many synagogues were entered through courtyards, a tradition which continued in the Diaspora and was also adopted by early Christian builders. The courtyard surely recalled the organization of the Temple and served to separate sacred from profane space.

Some synagogues may have had galleries. The Great Synagogue in Alexandria is believed to have been a galleried basilica, a plan that was unknown in Europe before the seventeenth century. Archaeological evidence offers no support for the theory that ancient synagogue galleries were meant for women only. Indeed, evidence suggests that women played an important part in the sponsorship and organization of many ancient synagogues, holding important community offices.

THE WHITE LIMESTONE SYNAGOGUE AT CAPERNUM, ISRAEL, IS AMONG THE MOST BEAUTIFUL AND BEST-PRESERVED BASILICA PLAN SYNAGOGUES, NOTED FOR ITS BOLD ARCHITECTURAL FORMS AND RICH AND DETAILED CARVED DECORATION.

Dura Europos

ANCIENT SYNAGOGUES were extensively decorated. At Dura Europos, the discovery of a synagogue in 1932 revealed that ancient Jews decorated their walls with biblical scenes.

The city, on the banks of the Euphrates and an important center located between the ancient Greco-Roman world and the Sassanian-Parthian east, was a multicultural melting pot. The city was destroyed in 264 C.E., but a significant portion of the synagogue was saved because of its location against the west city wall, which was widened in a last-ditch defensive effort. The interior of the synagogue was filled with rubble to thicken the wall, thus saving its extraordinary fresco decorations until archaeologists uncovered them in the twentieth century.

The synagogue presents an indirect passage through a series of spaces, leading from the public street through community rooms into the sanctuary proper. A painted ark niche culminates the route and is decorated with paintings of the Jerusalem Temple, the menorah, and a succinct but clear scene of the binding of Isaac. The almost square room is surrounded by benches, and all the walls are covered by magnificent paintings–decorative, narrative, and symbolic representations. Most of the scenes can be identified, and some include inscriptions to help. There is no obvious narrative sequence, and incidents from many books of the Bible are represented.

Just as the forms and details of the images borrow from classical and Eastern artistic styles, the emphasis on salvation (as opposed, for instance, to ethics, a favorite rabbinic topic) is similar to the message of contemporary late-antique mystery religions, including nascent Christianity.

BETH ALPHA

THROUGHOUT THE BYZANTINE period, synagogue floors were frequently covered with mosaic decorations, many of them consisting of geometric and vegetal designs, but some areas also contained panels enclosing symbolic or even narrative scenes. This is fully expressed at the sixth-century synagogue of Beth Alpha in Israel's Jezreel Valley and in the recently discovered fifth-century synagogue at Sepphoris, also in Israel.

At Beth Alpha the worshiper crosses four distinct zones of decoration in the central aisle on the way to the ark. In the first, near the door, two lions flank a dedicatory inscription. Next is an unusually narrative scene depicting the binding of Isaac, a central story in Jewish lore, signifying the special covenant between God and the Jews. This is followed by a large square panel with a zodiac wheel, portraying the months and zodiac signs. In the four corners are representations of the seasons, depicted as Classically garbed human figures. In the center is a charioteer reining four horses. In the pagan world, this is a device used to represent Helios, the sun god, but here the meaning may be more general: the sun as the center of the cosmos, all of which is God's creation.

The fourth zone, immediately in front of the ark niche, depicts a series of Jewish symbols–ark, menorah, *lulav*, *ethrog*, shofar–that are associated with the Jerusalem Temple and the festivals that had been celebrated there. Here is an indication that the synagogue serves as a replacement (albeit temporary) for the destroyed central sanctuary. Recent finds in synagogues of pieces of metal menorahs, similar in design to the Temple type, suggest that menorahs may sometimes have been employed in the service.

Opposite: THE SYNAGOGUE AT SARDIS, TURKEY, THE LARGEST ANCIENT ONE EXCAVATED, IS SITUATED ON THE FORMER MAIN ROAD OF THE LYDIAN CAPITAL, AMIDST AN ASSEMBLAGE OF ROMAN PUBLIC BUILDINGS. ITS SIZE AND LOCATION BESPEAK THE AFFLUENCE AND PROMINENCE OF THE CITY'S JEWISH COMMUNITY IN THE FOURTH CENTURY C.E. INSIDE, TWO AEDICULAE, ONE OF WHICH IS SEEN HERE, FLANK THE ENTRANCE. DESPITE THEIR UNUSUAL LOCATION, THESE WERE ARKS TO HOLD THE TORAH SCROLLS. *Above, top:* THIS DETAIL FROM THE COMPLEX PAINTED WALL DECORATION OF THE THIRD-CENTURY DURA EUROPOS SYNAGOGUE DEPICTS A REPRESENTATION OF THE TEMPLE OF JERUSALEM, SEEN HERE AS A TYPICAL GREEK STRUCTURE SURROUNDED BY COLUMNS. *Above, bottom:* AT THE SIXTH-CENTURY SYNA-GOGUE AT BETH ALPHA, ISRAEL, THE MOSAIC FLOOR IS RICHLY LAID WITH SYMBOLIC AND NARRATIVE DECORATION, INCLUDING THIS ROUNDEL SET WITHIN A DEPICTION OF THE ZODIAC. SURPRISINGLY, THE IMAGE IS OF HELIOS, THE PAGAN SUN GOD, POSSIBLY MEANT TO REPRESENT THE COSMOS IN THIS JEWISH CONTEXT.

TUCKED AWAY

Synagogues in
the Middle Ages

Lᴏᴜᴛᴛʟᴇ ɪs ᴋɴᴏᴡɴ ᴀʙᴏᴜᴛ sʏɴᴀɢᴏɢᴜᴇs
during the nearly 500 years between the decline of ancient Rome and
the rise of medieval towns. Hundreds of towns and cities throughout
Europe in the early Middle Ages surely had small Jewish populations,
but most of these communities had no synagogues. Various
prohibitions against building new synagogues were in force throughout
Christian Europe. Nevertheless, some new synagogues were built,
though most were small in size, discreet in location, and
susceptible to sudden closure by zealous Christian authorities.

SYNAGOGUES IN PRIVATE HOUSES

MEDIEVAL SYNAGOGUES were usually modest in size and most often located within or adjacent to the house or business of the richest Jews, who served as patrons or sponsors for their brethren.

The defining characteristics of these synagogues were primarily their furnishings, now long gone. Nonetheless, documentary evidence, occasionally manuscript illuminations, and lucky archaeological and architectural finds help to create a general picture. There is physical evidence, too.

A fine stone townhouse in the medieval Italian town of Sermoneta has been identified as a former synagogue. Worshipers must have met in a large well-lit room on the first floor, a space traditionally reserved as a reception room or bedroom for the master of the house.

An idea of what the interior arrangement of such a domestic synagogue space might have looked like can be gleaned from a fifteenth-century Italian manuscript illustration that shows an open room with a tall wooden ark set against one wall and a lower reader's table set before it. To either side of the room are chests or desks at which the worshipers sit, facing the center of the room. On each desk is a prayer book (*siddur*) and a candle burning in a candlestick. This is a night service; it is dark outside the four Romanesque-style double-light windows. The room is elegant, with a large decorated arch supported on Corinthian columns, which in turn support a wooden coffered ceiling. Each ceiling coffer is decorated with a painted star. The floor is made of red ceramic tile. Rooms like this can still be found in Early Renaissance *palazzi* throughout Italy.

Pages 28-29: THE LARGE SIZE AND FINE BRICKWORK OF TOLEDO'S FOURTEENTH-CENTURY HALEVI ABULAFIA SYNAGOGUE INDICATE THE WEALTH AND PRESTIGE OF ITS FOUNDER, COURTIER SAMUEL HALEVI ABULAFIA. *Page 29, detail:* A DETAIL FROM A DOORWAY OF THE ALTNEUSHUL IN PRAGUE. *Above:* THE REMU SYNAGOGUE, BUILT IN THE HEART OF CRACOW'S JEWISH TOWN, KNOWN AS KAZIMIERZ, IN 1556–7, IS BELIEVED TO BE THE FIRST POLISH MASONRY SYNAGOGUE BUILT IN THE RENAISSANCE STYLE. IT WAS A PRIVATE SYNAGOGUE FOUNDED BY THE MERCHANT ISRAEL BEN JOZEF ISSERLES, AND IT IS BEST KNOWN FOR ITS ASSOCIATION WITH ISRAEL'S SON RABBI MOSES ISSERLES, KNOWN AS THE REMU, ONE OF POLAND'S GREATEST JEWISH LEGAL SCHOLARS. *Opposite:* ATTACHED TO THE MEDIEVAL SYNAGOGUE IN WORMS, GERMANY, IS A SMALL STUDY ROOM. THOUGH IT IS CALLED THE "RASHI CHAPEL" AFTER THE RENOWNED MEDIEVAL SAGE WHO STUDIED IN WORMS FOR A TIME, THE ROOM ACTUALLY DATES FROM THE 1620S AND WAS A GIFT OF THE WEALTHY DAVID OPPENHEIMER, LONG AFTER RASHI'S TIME.

Throughout much of the Middle Ages, communities continued to interpret Jewish worship along local lines. In architecture, this usually meant relying on local, non-Jewish building and design traditions. The Jewish communities of northern (and eventually eastern) Europe came to be known as Ashkenazic, distinguished by the use of the Yiddish language—a mixture of Hebrew and German—specific pronunciations of Hebrew, and preferences in ritual and even synagogue architecture.

THIS HISTORIC PHOTOGRAPH SHOWS THE WORMS SYNAGOGUE BEFORE IT WAS DESTROYED BY THE NAZIS IN 1938 AND FURTHER LEVELED BY ALLIED BOMBING DURING WORLD WAR II. BENCHES CROWD AROUND THE CENTRAL READER'S TABLE, AND THE SPACE IS LIT BY CANDLES. TWO LARGE POINTED ARCHES AT LEFT GIVE ACCESS TO THE WOMEN'S SECTION, ADDED IN 1213 BUT FULLY JOINED TO THE MAIN HALL ONLY IN THE NINETEENTH CENTURY.

ENGLISH SYNAGOGUES

A NUMBER OF JEWISH communities built substantial synagogues in England before the Jews were expelled from the country in 1290. The synagogues are known, for the most part, from passing references, though many survived and were subsequently used as churches.

A Jewish community in Oxford is recorded as early as 1075, and there are documentary references to its synagogue. In London, where the earliest synagogues were within the city, both St. Stephen's and St. Mary, Colechurch were initially synagogues until they were confiscated and handed over to the Church.

Before the expulsion, the favorable years for the Jews in England in the early part of the reign of Henry I encouraged them to embark on the construction of a "magnificent" house of worship in London, probably to replace other humbler houses of prayer already in the city. When the building was complete, it aroused envy and hostility. The king was petitioned for its confiscation, which was granted in 1232, when the new building and its outbuildings were consecrated to the Virgin and given to the Brethren of St. Anthony of Vienna, from which the name St. Anthony's Hospital was eventually derived.

Old Jewry, a street in London, had a place of worship on its northeast corner, which was also confiscated and granted to the Order of the Sackcloth Friars, who had complained about the "howling of the Jews at prayer." This was but one of a number of synagogues, many in private houses, that were subjected to confiscation and suppression from the year 1232 until the expulsion in 1290.

In January 1996, the Guildford Museum Excavation Unit in Guildford, England, announced the uncovering of a building, dated circa 1180, beneath a High Street property— perhaps the remains of a medieval synagogue. It consisted of a small room, about ten feet (3m) square, built of chalk with a stone bench running around the room. East and west walls have blind arcades, and north and south have plainer recesses and doorways. A niche on the east side may have housed an ark. Scorch marks on the pilaster to one side of this recess may be from the *ner tamid* (eternal light). Pottery in the rubble fill dates the destruction of the building to around 1270.

SOPRON, HUNGARY, SYNAGOGUES

M ORE PUBLIC AND LAVISH versions of the hall-plan type of synagogue did exist, and a few such buildings are known, including fragments of two synagogues in Sopron, Hungary. The thirteenth-century synagogue of Sopron is among the best preserved and has been partially reconstructed.

Sopron was a royal and important western border town. The Jewish community was small—ten to sixteen households—with few rich members. The synagogue was used every day for religious worship, and also for judicial and commercial purposes. The primary building was set back from the street and reached via a passageway between two houses. One enters the northern part of the synagogue through a narrow corridor. The floor of the sanctuary is three steps lower than the vestibule. The sanctuary is an open vaulted space with the ark set into the eastern wall and adorned with carved stonework–clusters of grapes and grape leaves surmounted by a Star of David. The grape garlands are painted blue and brown, and the top is maroon. Three stairs to the ark are flanked by ornamental piers.

The prayer room for women had a separate entrance on the south. It led to a narrow courtyard between tall walls. On the synagogue lot were other structures, including a caretaker's house, a narrow building built toward the end of the fourteenth century to house travelers or the sick, and a *mikvah,* or Jewish ritual bath.

On the other side of the street is a second medieval synagogue, like the first in design but with no separate women's room and no front entrance. It is thought that this was a private synagogue built by a banker named Israel in the fourteenth century. Sopron's Jews were often persecuted, and were finally expelled in 1526. The synagogues were closed and partially demolished.

Synagogues of Worms and Regensburg, Germany

In towns with larger Jewish populations and greater resources, synagogues larger and more architecturally ambitious than those of Sopron were erected. Foremost among these are a series of double-nave structures built across central Europe beginning in the twelfth century. A few of these buildings survive, and much is known about others that have been destroyed.

The medieval synagogue of Worms has been rebuilt, damaged, and repaired many times since its founding in 1034. The current double-nave plan reflects the interior arrangement at the end of the twelfth century. This photograph, taken from the doorway looking into the main sanctuary, demonstrates that the best sight lines are on the diagonal.

west on the same side as the women's annex, was not disturbed. The so-called Rashi Chapel, added in 1624, is at the short western end of the building. A mikvah, built around 1186, was a separate structure southwest of the synagogue.

The twin-nave plan was also used for the Regensburg synagogue, demolished in 1519 but recorded in a pair of etchings made shortly before it was destroyed. One shows the prayer hall, the other the vestibule. Archaeological excavation in 1996 revealed the foundations of this building. According to the etchings, there were three columns on the synagogue's east-west axis, with the bimah–a low platform, only three steps above floor level–between the second and third columns. The reader's desk was slightly to the right. The bimah enclosure is in the Renaissance style, representative of the new style appearing in Germany at that time.

THE ALTNEUSHUL OF PRAGUE

THE OLDEST SYNAGOGUE in continuous use in Europe is Prague's Altneushul (Old-New Synagogue), built in the late thirteenth century. The Altneushul, a double-nave, Gothic building about 49 × 29 feet (15 × 9m),

Left: THE GOTHIC ARCHITECTURE OF PRAGUE'S ALTNEUSHUL IS TYPICAL OF ITS TIME. THE THICK WALLS PIERCED BY SMALL WINDOWS CARRY THE MASONRY VAULTED CEILING. THE ORIGINAL BUILDING IS SURROUNDED BY ANNEXES WHICH ENLARGE THE SPACE (ESPECIALLY FOR WOMEN) AND ALSO SERVE AS STRUCTURAL BUTTRESSES. *Opposite:* THE INTERIOR OF THE ALTNEUSHUL IS A COMPACT SPACE DIVIDED INTO TWIN NAVES AND SURMOUNTED BY HIGH RIB VAULTS SUPPORTED BY TWO OCTAGONAL PIERS. IN THE CENTER IS THE LATE GOTHIC BIMAH (PROBABLY BUILT AFTER A POGROM IN 1483) ENCLOSED BY ITS IRON GRILLE, OVER WHICH HANGS A BANNER GIVEN TO PRAGUE'S JEWISH COMMUNITY BY EMPEROR CHARLES IV IN 1358 AND RESTORED IN THE EIGHTEENTH CENTURY.

Of these, the synagogue at Worms, Germany, is one of the most impressive. The Worms synagogue consists of several sections built in different periods, and all rebuilt after being destroyed during World War II. The original building was constructed in 1034 and rebuilt for the first time using the twin-nave plan in 1175, when the men's hall was built. The hall of worship was divided by two columns into two parallel aisles of equal size. The ark stood at the eastern end; the bimah was in the center between the columns. A women's annex was added in 1213. The old Romanesque portal of the synagogue, farther

Above: THE EXTERIOR OF THE STARY (OLD) SYNAGOGUE IN CRACOW, POLAND, APPEARS FORTIFIED, REMINDING US THAT WHEN IT WAS BUILT IN THE LATE FIFTEENTH CENTURY, SYN-
AGOGUES WERE AMONG THE ONLY MASONRY BUILDINGS IN JEWISH DISTRICTS. THEY COULD BE USED AS PLACES OF REFUGE FOR JEWS IN TIMES OF VIOLENCE, OR THEY COULD SERVE
IN THE TOWN'S DEFENSE DURING ATTACKS OR INVASIONS. THIS VIEW SHOWS THE SYNAGOGUE'S PLACEMENT ON SZEROKA (BROAD) STREET AND THE ATTACHED ANNEX FOR WOMEN.
Opposite: THE STARY SYNAGOGUE USES THE MEDIEVAL DOUBLE-NAVE PLAN BUT RECREATES IT IN A LIGHT MODE. REBUILT BY THE ITALIAN RENAISSANCE ARCHITECT MATTEO GUCCI
AROUND 1480, THE SYNAGOGUE HAS AN OPEN, AIRY QUALITY UNKNOWN IN EARLIER MEDIEVAL DESIGNS.

is divided lengthwise by two octagonal piers. The bimah stands between the piers; its wrought-iron enclosure with pointed arches is presumed to date to the fifteenth century. The ark, with its classical columns supported on volute brackets, dates from the sixteenth century. The old, beautifully carved Gothic gable that was part of the original ark has

been fitted into the modern one, creating a harmony of old and new.

The synagogue is surrounded by a number of low annexes added throughout its history. The earliest addition to the structure is the vestibule on the south side, which contains the entrance. The west annex was added in the seventeenth century; the north annex was rebuilt

in 1731. Narrow windows about three feet (1m) above the floor level connect the women's annex with the main hall. A corridor at the east side, added in the late 1700s, was partially removed in a recent restoration. The main part of the synagogue's present-day appearance dates to a restoration of 1716. It was repaired again in 1883, in 1921–26, and in 1966–67.

Above and opposite: THE GREAT SYNAGOGUE OF TOLEDO IS THE MOST IMPRESSIVE SPANISH JEWISH MONUMENT. ITS FIVE AISLES, SEPARATED BY ROWS OF OCTAGONAL PIERS SURMOUNTED BY HORSESHOE ARCHES, CREATE A SPACIOUS INTERIOR. THE ARCHES, AND OTHER MOTIFS EVIDENT IN THE STUCCO WORK, WERE REVIVED IN JEWISH ARCHITECTURE IN NINETEENTH-CENTURY SYNAGOGUES THROUGHOUT EUROPE AND THE UNITED STATES.

THE TOLEDO SYNAGOGUES

IN MEDIEVAL SPAIN a separate tradition developed, more dependent upon eastern Jewish authorities and Muslim cultural influences in the creation of a liturgical, linguistic, and artistic tradition. The Iberian peninsula was called Sepheras by Jews. What has come to be known as Sephardic culture first developed in what is now Spain and Portugal and was later exported throughout the world due to the migrations of the expelled Iberian Jewish population.

In the twelfth century there were more than 12,000 Jews in Toledo, Spain. The city, with nine synagogues and five small chapels, was often called "the Jerusalem of Spain." Today, two important synagogues from this period still survive, both now National Monuments. The older of the two was originally the Great Synagogue but is now commonly known as Santa Maria la Blanca, after the church into which it was transformed following the expulsion of the Jews in 1492.

The exterior is modest, but inside the four rows of thirty-two octagonal piers, which support horseshoe arches, articulate an impressive free-flowing open space. Elaborate stucco ornamentation in the clerestory windows gives a semblance of original decorative opulence. The interior is 92 feet (28m) long, 75 feet (23m) wide, and 41 feet (12.5m) high. The carved plaster capitals are decorated with pinecone motifs.

The other Toledo synagogue that survives was built as a private palace chapel by Samuel HaLevi Abulafia, who was treasurer and close adviser to King Pedro I. In 1357 Pedro granted Abulafia permission to build the synagogue for his family, but in 1361, the king turned against his adviser, and Abulafia was imprisoned and tortured to death.

The synagogue, commonly called El Transito, is known for its rich stucco decoration, which includes Hebrew inscriptions encircling the nave

Above: In Cordova, the birthplace of the Jewish sage Maimonides, there survives an earlier private synagogue built by Isaac Menhab in 1314–15. Much smaller than HaLevi Abulafia's synagogue, it is also richly decorated with painted stucco. An inscription says that Menhab built "This lesser sanctuary...as a temporary abode. Hasten O god, to rebuild Jerusalem." *Opposite:* The private synagogue of Samuel HaLevi Abulafia is commonly known as El Transito—a nonsensical amalgam of Christian and Jewish designations. Behind the three arches in the sumptuously decorated eastern wall was a hechal for the Torah scrolls.

just below the intricately designed and richly decorated ceiling. The synagogue was connected to Abulafia's palace on its east side. While some inscriptions praise King Pedro I, others hail Abulafia as "prince among the princes of the tribe of Levi." Architecturally the synagogue is a monument to the court style of Pedro I, and bears the king's coat of arms and testimony of his greatness. The building owes as much to the tradition of Christian royal or noble chapels as to any known synagogue prototypes.

The synagogue is an open rectangular sanctuary of comparatively large proportions: about 76 feet (23m) by 31 feet (9.5m) and 39 feet (12m) high. It has a spacious women's gallery on the north side and a gallery along the western wall that is thought to have been the choir loft. The eastern wall–where the Torah scrolls were located–is encrusted with decorative panels dominated by a rectangular windowed niche, in front of which stand three foliated columns on slim colonettes.

The synagogue is covered with remarkably well-preserved stucco relief of extraordinary quality with geometric patterns and interlacing, together with floral rinceau and cartouches, blind arcades, and heraldic shields. Above the galleries runs a broad ornamental frieze, and above this is an arcade of windows and blind arches. The arrangement along the eastern wall, however, is completely different. Two windows are set side by side in the center, suggesting in both shape and position the twin tablets of the law. The ceiling, made of cedar of Lebanon, is decorated with Hebrew calligraphy. The decorations on the walls include Hebrew passages from the Bible.

Following the death of Abulafia, it appears that the great age of synagogue building in Sepheras ended. Conditions for Jews deteriorated as Christian hegemony in the peninsula increased. Anti-Jewish feeling increased and led to widespread anti-Jewish riots in 1391, the forced conversion of many Jews, and confiscation of Jewish property.

In the next century, the use of synagogues was strictly controlled until, in 1492, all Jews were expelled from Spain.

EMERGING ELEGANCE

From Renaissance to Emancipation

AFTER THE EXPULSION OF THE JEWS FROM SPAIN
in 1492, many Sephardic exiles settled in Italy, especially in the trading
centers of Ancona and Venice and the new port of Livorno, established
by the Medici dukes of Tuscany. Jews had lived in Italy since antiquity,
and during the Middle Ages there had been small Jewish
populations throughout the peninsula. From the sixteenth century on,
these communities built impressive synagogues. The structures were
still modest on the outside, but within they were lavishly decorated.

Pages 42–43: THE POLISH SYNAGOGUE AT LANCUT, BUILT IN 1761, IS A FINE SURVIVING EXAMPLE OF A BAROQUE SYNAGOGUE. THE FOUR-COLUMN BIMAH BOTH HELPS DEFINE THE SPACE AND SUPPORT THE MASONRY CEILING VAULT. THE BRILLIANT POLYCHROME DECORATIONS HAVE BEEN RECENTLY RESTORED—HERE ONE SEES DELIGHTFUL DEPICTIONS OF BIBLICAL SCENES INCLUDING THE TEMPTATION OF EVE (RIGHT) AND THE BINDING OF ISAAC (LEFT). *Page 43, detail:* A CARVED RELIEF MENORAH ADDS TO THE BEAUTY OF THE OLD SYNAGOGUE IN CRACOW, POLAND. *Above and opposite:* MANY OF THE SYNAGOGUES IN THE VENETIAN GHETTO WERE HARD TO FIND AND WERE LOCATED IN THE UPPERMOST STORIES OF TALL RESIDENTIAL BUILDINGS. ONLY THE ROWS OF TALL ARCHED WINDOWS INDICATE THE PRESENCE OF THE SIXTEENTH-CENTURY SCUOLA GRANDE TEDESCA BEHIND THESE WALLS. INSIDE, GREAT CARE AND EXPENSE WERE LAVISHED ON THE SANCTUARY. THE GILDED WOODEN ARK, WITH SIDE SEATS FOR ELDERS OF THE SYNAGOGUE, AND THE ELLIPTICAL WOMEN'S GALLERY ABOVE DATE FROM EIGHTEENTH-CENTURY RESTORATIONS.

SYNAGOGUES OF VENICE

THE FINEST SYNAGOGUES of this period, which extends through the eighteenth century, are in the Venice Ghetto, where five separate synagogues survive and have recently been restored to their earlier splendor.

In 1516 Jewish residency was formalized with the establishment of the "Ghetto Nuovo" in Venice—an area allocated to Italian Jews and merchant Jews from northern Europe who followed the Ashkenazic rite. While it provided for the separation of Jews form the Christian community and thereby "protected" the latter from the purported bad religious and social influence Jews were believed to exert, it also enforced a greater cohesion within the Jewish community, which was certainly a factor in the creation of Venice's vibrant Jewish culture in the sixteenth through eighteenth centuries. Primary to the expression of this culture was the erection and decoration of a series of beautiful synagogues.

Scuola Grande Tedesca

The Scuola Grande Tedesca was built in 1528–29 and rebuilt in 1732–33. The synagogue is located high up in a tall building. The location removed the synagogue as much as possible form the tumult of everyday life and also protected it from vandalism. Perhaps most important, the upstairs location allowed the synagogue builders to follow, as much as possible, the Talmudic dictum that the synagogue should be located at the highest point in town.

The sanctuary space is two stories high and trapezoidal in shape. It has an elliptical gallery for women inserted at the second level, a result of eighteenth-century modernizing remodeling, which creates an intimate atmosphere reminiscent of contemporary theater buildings. The rich gilding on the woodwork of the gallery, ark, and bimah must have been especially evocative in the days before electricity. Originally, the bimah was probably located in the center of the space, but by the time the synagogue was remodeled, the Sephardic bipolar plan, which placed bimah and ark at opposite ends of the prayer hall, was favored in Venice and, as we shall see, elsewhere in Italy.

Scuola Canton

The Scuola Canton was built in 1531–32 and rebuilt with a new ark in 1672. This small rectangular space is one of the world's most elegant synagogues, and a restoration completed in the 1980s has reopened blocked windows and returned to the space the light, color, and delicate ornamentation so reminiscent of a Venetian patrician's parlor or the meeting place of Christian confraternity.

Passing through a narrow vestibule (over which is a women's gallery) the synagogue is entered along a long wall. Bright light from large windows, curtained in red, shines over the ark and bimah, set across from each other in the bipolar plan. Benches line the long sides of the room, and congregants would follow the service by looking first to the left, then to the right, as at a tennis match, but here, instead of a ball, it is of course the word and melody of prayer that ricochets across the space.

The ark, built in 1736, is made of richly carved and gilded wood, typical of Italian synagogues of the Baroque period. Its size, however, harmonizes with the intimate Renaissance space. The bimah, dated 1780, is set in a raised niche that protrudes from the building and overhangs a canal. It is surmounted by a little cupola, allowing heavenly light to aid the Torah reader, and is framed with columns intricately carved as intertwined branches and twigs.

The Ghetto Vecchio

In 1541, the influx of Jewish refugees from Spain and Portugal via the Ottoman Empire settled in the Ghetto Vecchio, an area adjacent to the original ghetto enclosure. In this new

Opposite: THE SUMPTUOUS INTERIOR OF THE SCUOLA GRANDE SPAGNOLA IS A MIX OF RICH MARBLES, WOODS, METALS, AND TEXTILES. TYPICAL OF MANY SEPHARDIC SYNAGOGUES, THE BENCHES ARE ARRANGED ALONG A CENTRAL AXIS BETWEEN ARK AND BIMAH, WHICH FACE EACH OTHER FROM OPPOSITE ENDS OF THE ROOM. *Above:* IN THE GHETTO VECCHIO THE SEPHARDIC JEWS FROM SPAIN AND PORTUGAL ERECTED IMPOSING SYNAGOGUES, EMPLOYING PROMINENT VENETIAN ARCHITECTS. THE ORNATE FACADE OF THE SCUOLA LEVANTINA IS ATTRIBUTED BY MANY TO THE PROMINENT SEVENTEENTH-CENTURY VENETIAN ARCHITECT BALDASSARE LONGHENA.

only by distinctive window patterns, the rich material and lavish exterior architectural details of these new buildings were meant to be seen and admired.

Of the two synagogues, the Scuola Grande Spagnola is the more magnificent. A bipolar arrangement of ark and bimah is set within the large rectangular space, and an elliptical gallery for women is inserted high up the elevation of the tall room. The entire interior is sumptuously decorated with black and white marbles, rich woods, and faux-marble wall painting. The exuberant ark design of rising classical elements culminates in a series of pediments and arches set within one another, typical of Longhena's style. Within this composition are the Ten Commandments mounted on a frame of golden rays, the same device used by Gian Lorenzo Bernini to frame the elevated chair of St. Peter in St. Peter's Basilica in Rome.

FRANCE

RELATED TO THE ITALIAN synagogues are two remarkable buildings in southern France. Jews of Provence were not expelled in the Middle Ages because this region was independent, ruled directly by the popes. In succeeding centuries Jewish communities continued in the area, and in the eighteenth century Jews in Carpentras and Cavaillon redesigned their synagogues in the latest decorative fashion emanating from the Royal Court.

Thus, in these Sephardic synagogues, we find a taste of Versailles in the delicate frothy rococo decoration. The Carpentras synagogue, originally built in 1367, was remodeled in 1741 by architect Antoine d'Alemand. The Cavaillon synagogue was rebuilt in 1772 by master masons Antoine Armelin and his son Pierre.

area, two major new synagogues were erected—the Scuola Levantina (built after 1589, remodeled in the seventeenth century) and the Scuola Grande Spagnola (also built after 1589, remodeled in the mid-seventeenth century).

Workshops of Venice's most prominent architects, most likely including Baldassare Longhena, were employed for these synagogues, which were grander than the earlier prayer houses. Still within the enclosed Ghetto, they were nonetheless visible to the population at large as signs of Jewish wealth and taste. Unlike the synagogues on top floors of apartment buildings, recognizable from the outside

HOLLAND AND ITS COLONIES

ASECOND AREA of intensive synagogue building was the new Dutch Republic and those parts of the world settled by Dutch traders. Jews settled in all these new commercial centers, where they were allowed relative freedom of worship and work, and for those who came from Spanish and Portuguese territories, there was the opportunity to renounce the Christianity which had been forced upon them or their parents and to embrace (albeit often in ignorance) traditional Judaism.

These communities, closely tied to the new Sephardic trading communities of Italy and the Ottoman Empire, incorporated traditional Jewish worship needs and aspirations with more Catholic artistic taste. Thus buildings were erected on a grand scale, and the cemeteries of these communities are filled with richly carved gravestones sporting typically Italian and Spanish Baroque motifs.

The Amsterdam Esnoga

In 1670, in Amsterdam, the Portuguese community studied projects for the enlargement of their synagogue, also called an *esnoga*. They decided to build a spacious and grandiose place of worship with offices, a library, and schoolrooms on a site donated by 650 members

of the congregation. A plan by Amsterdam master builder Elias Bouman was selected–a restrained interpretation of the classical style, already familiar in contemporary Protestant buildings. Described as dignified, sedate, and serene, the style is opulent though without any of the drama of the Italian Baroque style.

Four cornerstones were laid in April 1671, and the work took four years to complete. The synagogue was dedicated in 1675 in a ceremony with choir and orchestra followed by six days of celebrations. At that time it was the largest synagogue in the world. The Dutch artist Romeyn de Hooghe extolled the building in a poem as "the glory of the Amstel and its senate" and designed a commemorative broadside with allegorical figures representing the Dutch Republic, freedom of conscience, and the High Priest with the Scroll of the Law posing benignly on clouds above the nave of the new esnoga.

The hall (125 × 95 feet [38 × 29m]) seats over 1,200 men, and more than 400 women can be seated in the galleries. Four giant Ionic columns on massive plinths on either side support the barrel-vaulted ceiling. Six smaller columns support the galleries, which run about three sides of the building. The ark and bimah are impressive works of Brazilian jacaranda wood. The ark is surmounted by pediments, crowns, and obelisks; above the central bay, in an aedicule beneath a crowned pediment, are the Tables of the Law. The esnoga's seventy-two windows ensure bright light, and at evening hundreds of candles on magnificent chandeliers and in candlesticks on each bench light up the interior.

Around the spacious courtyard is a group of ancillary buildings including a school, community offices, the rabbinate, and the famous Etz Hayim Library, which continues to retain its seventeenth-century appearance.

ENGLAND

JEWS HAD BEEN EXPELLED from England in 1290 and returned with the consent of Oliver Cromwell in 1656.

At first, London Jews rented a house with the rabbi's residence on the ground floor and the prayer hall above, with women in an adjoining room. A Christian visitor described them "in rich silks daubed with broad gold lace, with muffs on one hand and books in the other." The synagogue became one of the sights of London and the stream of Christian visitors provoked the following ordinance: "To avoid the scandal and hindrance caused when English ladies come to see the ceremonies of our religion, it is forbidden and ordained that no member of the Holy Congregation may bring them to it, nor rise nor move from his place to receive them."

The effect of Amsterdam's synagogue was widely felt. In England, Bevis Marks Synagogue, built in 1701 by England's new Sephardic community, recalls the Amsterdam esnoga in its red brick exterior and interior plan (80 × 50 feet [24.5 × 15m]). The ark,

however, resembles the altars of London. The Ashkenazim of London built their first synagogue in 1722, in Duke's Place, near Bevis Marks, and another, the Hambro Synagogue, in 1725 in Fenchurch Street, also in the city. Both were modeled on the Bevis Marks building.

THE NEW WORLD

DUTCH AND ENGLISH Jews, inspired by the Amsterdam and London synagogues, built structures in the New World, where many of them had settled.

Jews from Amsterdam settled in Curaçao in 1659, headed by a man who had brought a Torah scroll with him. The synagogue they built is a four-story building standing in a tiled courtyard. A master carpenter was brought from Amsterdam to participate in the construction. The building shows the influence of both the Amsterdam esnoga and Spanish Baroque style. Other Caribbean synagogues were erected in Suriname, Barbados, Nevis, St. Eustatius, and St. Thomas.

In Newport, Rhode Island, Sephardic Jews commissioned architect Peter Harrison (1716–75), the first skilled architect in New England, to build a new synagogue. Harrison followed the many architectural model books available at the time. The synagogue, begun in 1759 and dedicated in 1763, is named after its first rabbi, Isaac Touro (d. 1784), and his sons, Abraham (d. 1822) and Judah (d. 1854), who were its benefactors. The rectangular hall, about 35 × 40 feet (11 × 12m), has two tiers of columns, the lower Ionic, the upper Corinthian, which support galleries on three sides and the ceiling. A balustrade runs around the gallery. The ark is set against the east wall. The interior, now painted in gray and white, was originally apple green, a favorite color for decoration in the Georgian period.

POLAND

In these same years, a very different sort of synagogue was becoming increasingly common in northern and eastern Europe.

Jews first settled in Cracow, Poland, in 1304. Legends date the Old Synagogue there to the fourteenth century, but it was probably first erected in the late fifteenth century and then rebuilt by the Italian architect Matteo Gucci in 1570. Renovated in 1936, it was ravaged shortly thereafter during the German occupation of Cracow, and then rebuilt in the 1950s as a museum.

Many of the Polish synagogues of the sixteenth through eighteenth centuries were designed by Italians, most of whom worked for the Polish nobility. They brought many spatial and decorative fashions to Poland from Italy, and, under noble patronage, these were adapted for Jewish use. The Old Synagogue is a transitional building, retaining its medieval two-nave plan, similar to the synagogues in both Worms and Prague, but incorporating many Renaissance features, including a lighter design, in its remodeling.

A substantial number of hall-type synagogues were erected over the next century throughout greater Poland. These included the famous and now destroyed Nachmanowiczes Synagogue (also known as TaZ Synagogue, or Golden Rose), built in 1582 in Lvov (now Lviv), Ukraine. A few of these buildings—such as those at Pinczow and Sydlow, Poland—survive as ruins or have been adapted to other uses. Pinczow's synagogue, built around 1600, is notable as one of the first Polish synagogues to include a women's section (situated over the vestibule) in its original design. Wall paintings from the second half of the eighteenth century, attributed to the Jewish painter Jehuda Leib, still decorate parts of this synagogue.

Opposite: Mikveh Israel Synagogue, built in 1732 in Curaçao, is the oldest synagogue in use in the New World. Its Sephardic bipolar plan and galleries were adapted from the Esnoga in Amsterdam to suit the smaller Caribbean community's needs. *Above:* The Pinkas Synagogue in Prague was built as a private synagogue for the prominent Horowitz family. It is noteworthy especially for the net vault over its single-naved main space, which probably dates from 1519, as undoubtedly did the original Gothic ark and Gothic-Renaissance bimah. In the early seventeenth century, the master builder Judah Coref de Herz vaulted the vestibule on the south and the ground-floor women's section, built the women's gallery, and remodeled the exterior. The bimah received its Rococo frame in 1798. The synagogue is now a monument to Czech victims of the Holocaust, whose names are inscribed on its walls.

Above: THE ARK OF THE SYNAGOGUE IN TYKOCIN, POLAND, SHOWS POLISH SYNAGOGUE DECORATION AT ITS MOST EXU-
BERANT. THE RESTORATION OF THIS MASSIVE SYNAGOGUE, BUILT IN 1642, IS ONLY PARTIAL. WE HAVE TO IMAGINE STEPS
THAT LED UP TO THE ARK AND A WOODEN CABINET FILLED WITH TORAH SCROLLS AND COVERED WITH A RICHLY EMBROI-
DERED CLOTH CURTAIN (*PAROCHET*). *Opposite:* FOR SEVERAL CENTURIES HUNDREDS OF MODEST SYNAGOGUES EXISTED IN
TOWNS AND VILLAGES THROUGHOUT GERMANY, OFTEN RESEMBLING LOCAL HOUSES AND SHOPS IN THEIR SIZE AND
ARCHITECTURAL STYLE, SUCH AS THIS HALF-TIMBERED SYNAGOGUE IN CELLE. UNLIKE BIG URBAN SYNAGOGUES, WHICH
WERE MOSTLY DESTROYED ON KRISTALLNACHT, MANY OF THE SMALLER BUILDINGS SURVIVED THE HOLOCAUST AND WERE
APPROPRIATED FOR NON-JEWISH USE IN THE POSTWAR PERIOD. NOW MANY OF THESE SYNAGOGUES ARE BEING IDENTI-
FIED AS SUCH, AND AS IN THE CASE OF THIS ONE IN CELLE, RESTORED.

A second important type of synagogue appears in Poland in the late sixteenth century. This type is defined by its square, or almost square, plan and the presence of a large bimah in the center, surrounded by four corner columns that rise all the way to the ceiling vault, which they help support. This synagogue type, often called the "bimah-support synagogue," offered the opportunity for wider roof spans and, therefore, larger uninterrupted interior spaces. The size of the space, as well as the attention given to the reader's platform, created a new dramatic effect. It is thought that the first such synagogue may have been the MaHaRSHal Synagogue, built in Lublin, Poland, in 1567, rebuilt in 1656. This was probably the first synagogue built on a square plan with a central bimah integrated into its scheme.

Another surviving (but ruinous) example was built in Przemysl (1592-95), for which the building permit, issued by the Cathedral Chap-ter, is known. It stipulated that the length, width, and height of the hall of worship were not to exceed 20 *lokci*, or about 42 feet (13m). Obviously, each measurement was used to its limit, and the result was a square plan. The prescribed height proved inadequate, and the Bishop Laurentius Gostycki conceded that "should the vault require it, the floor may be lowered by two or three lokci, so that the syn-agogue should be stately." According to the permit, the roof had to have a "low, Italian roof," or terrace roofs. Further, the permit specified a gutter and a masonry parapet; the parapet was a precaution against fire.

Other surviving examples in Poland can be found at Zamosc (c. 1600), Tykocin (1642), and Lancut (1761). The latter two have recently been restored, and Lancut now most clearly presents the Baroque form of a princely synagogue that still retains traditional Jewish folk motifs.

Jews settled in Lancut in the sixteenth century and over the centuries made their livings as merchants, shopkeepers, and innkeepers. The masonry synagogue building, about 60 × 50 feet (18 × 15m) in size, was built in 1761 just outside the grounds of the palace of Count Potocki, under whose aegis the Jews of the town resided. It has a simple plan, with a vestibule and a room on the entrance side and a main hall beyond. Women sat above the vestibule and reached their gallery by an external stairway. The exterior and interior surfaces were plastered and covered with painted decoration. Upon descending several steps from the vestibule, one sees the main prayer hall, lit by large windows. In the center stands the bimah, comprised of four large thick columns set on square bases supporting the central vault.

NEW STYLES

IN GERMANY, PARTICULARLY in urban centers from which Jews had often been barred, new synagogues were being erected in more fashionable styles. In Berlin, for example, the Heidereutergasse Synagogue (1712–14) closely resembled contemporary Protestant church architecture in its detailing and its spatial configuration. This adaptation to local styles had, as we have seen, a long tradition. The eighteenth-century synagogues in Germany, however, prefigure the widespread erection of synagogues in that country in the nineteenth century, where every effort was made to insert synagogue architecture into the cultural mainstream.

In Wörlitz, Germany, the Duke of Anhalt-Dessau built a synagogue in 1789–90. The round structure was built in an English garden setting with other attractions, including a Gothic-style house, a Temple of Flora, and a floating bridge, in a manner typical of

contemporary pleasure-park architecture. It looked distinctly like an ancient temple, and indeed, the architect, Friedrich Wilhelm von Erdmannsdorff (1736–1800), called the building the Temple of Vesta. It was popularly known as the Judentempel. Twelve pilasters decorated the exterior. One portal opposite the ark led into the main hall while another identical door led to a stair to the semicircular gallery supported by six Doric columns. The round windows were set high, and the entire structure was topped by a conical roof. There was even a ritual bath, with a stove to heat it, within the complex.

Similar attempts to have Jews adopt exotic styles were common throughout Germany in the early nineteenth century. The classical style was adopted at Wörlitz, and elsewhere, such as at Lunéville, France (1785-88), and Vienna, Austria, where the Seitenstettentempel was dedicated in 1826.

In addition, variations of Egyptian architecture, made popular through the conquests of Napoleon, were also promoted, as at Karlsruhe, Germany (1798; destroyed 1871). In Kassel, the local noble's desire for an Egyptian-style synagogue was successfully fought by the Jews themselves, who argued that Jews were slaves in Egypt, and therefore the style was historically inappropriate. The Kassel community went for a more staid Romanesque Revival style.

Eventually the quest for a uniquely Jewish architecture style, coupled with Christian needs to clearly identify Jewish monumental buildings as distinct from churches, led to new types of synagogues and new styles, including, after the 1840s, the popularization of the so-called Moorish style. Widespread emancipation of Jews throughout Europe at the end of the eighteenth and beginning of the nineteenth centuries created new occasions and opportunities for synagogue art and architecture.

Above: THE SUCHOWOLA SYNAGOGUE, BUILT IN THE SECOND HALF OF THE EIGHTEENTH CENTURY, WAS A FINE EXAMPLE OF POLAND'S WOODEN SYNAGOGUES. AN OCTAGONAL SANCTUARY SPACE WAS SURROUNDED ON THREE SIDES BY A VESTIBULE AND SECTIONS FOR WOMEN. THE MAIN SPACE WAS SURMOUNTED BY A WOODEN VAULT, THE PRESENCE OF WHICH IS HINTED AT IN THIS EXTERIOR VIEW. *Opposite:* WHILE MOST OF THE WOODEN SYNAGOGUES OF POLAND HAVE BEEN DESTROYED, A FEW MODEST ONES CAN BE FOUND IN OUT-OF-THE-WAY PLACES, SUCH AS PIETRA NEAMT, ROMANIA. HERE, THE BA'AL SHEM TOV SYNAGOGUE MAINTAINS THE WARM INTIMACY OF SHTETL ARCHITECTURE. THOUGH BUILT IN THE NINETEENTH CENTURY, THE STRUCTURE RECALLS SYNAGOGUES OF EARLIER TIMES. IT IS BUILT HALFWAY UNDERGROUND TO CONFORM TO REGULATIONS THAT FORBADE SYNAGOGUES FROM BEING TALLER THAN SURROUNDING CHRISTIAN BUILDINGS.

Wooden Synagogues

While expensive masonry synagogues, such as that in Lancut, were springing up throughout greater Poland (the quarrying and transport of stone were usually more expensive than the actual construction), a parallel tradition developed of building synagogues in wood. Few of these buildings survive today; many were destroyed in World War I, the rest in 1939 or shortly thereafter, during World War II. Drawings and photographs, however, have preserved something of this remarkable legacy.

Wooden synagogues often preceded masonry ones; the wooden ones were replaced after a fire or when a community had the financial means. Wooden synagogues, however, could be magnificent in their own right and were frequently architecturally imaginative. Interiors especially, which favored central plans and high multiform cupolas, must have been emotionally charged places to pray. One of the most magnificent of these buildings was the synagogue at Wolpa (also Volpa), Poland, from the early eighteenth century.

Wooden synagogues (like their masonry contemporaries) were often covered inside with painted decoration, providing large commissions for Jewish folk artists. Surviving photographs and a few paintings give some impression of what has been lost. At Chodorow, Ukraine, the walls and ceiling are covered with multicolored painting. The synagogue in nearby Gwozdziec, Ukraine, has similarly decorated walls, which were painted in 1652. An early series in Germany decorated by Eliezer Sussman includes buildings from Bechhofen (1733) and Horb (1735), Unterlimpurg (1739) and Kirchheim (1739-40). The Horb synagogue's painted wooden ceiling is now in the Israel Museum.

Left: Vienna's Seitenstettengasse Synagogue, with its elegant interior arranged in an unusual elliptical plan, was designed by Josef Kornhausel and dedicated in 1826. It is the only synagogue in the Austrian capital not destroyed on Kristallnacht, in November 1938. The building is set within a larger urban block because of laws at the time of its construction that required non-Christian religious buildings to be invisible from the street; thus it was protected from the Nazi-inspired destruction. The only sign of the building's Jewish identity is the Tablets of the Law set above the ark. *Above, top:* Not far from Vienna is the Czech town of Mikulov, formerly Nikolsburg, for centuries a center of Moravian Jewry. The old synagogue was built in 1550 and totally remodeled in 1723. Its intimate interior is marked by a four-column bimah of remarkably delicate proportions. This is the same plan used in big Polish synagogues to the north but with an entirely different aesthetic. This view, looking up from the center of the bimah, reveals the richly decorated and recently restored vaulted ceiling. *Above, bottom:* The lovely Baroque synagogue at Mad, Hungary, was built in 1795 and overlooks the former Jewish section of this wine-producing town. The interior is inspired by traditional Polish synagogues.

PROSPERITY

*Synagogues in the
Muslim World*

❧

THE OLDEST KNOWN SYNAGOGUES
are found in countries that subsequently fell
under Muslim rule, and where Arab populations, or
at least Arabic culture, came to dominate. The spread of
Islam across much of Asia incorporated more
Jewish communities into the Muslim world, and for much
of the last millennium, the majority of the world's
Jews lived under Muslim rule.

Pages 58-59: THE EARLIEST REFERENCE TO THE BEN EZRA SYNAGOGUE IN CAIRO IS FROM 1106, BUT THE ORIGINAL SYN-AGOGUE WAS BUILT OVER TWO CENTURIES EARLIER AND DEMOLISHED IN 1013 WHEN ALL CHURCHES AND SYNAGOGUES IN EGYPT WERE ORDERED DESTROYED. REBUILT FROM 1039 TO 1041 ON A TRADITIONAL BASILICA PLAN, IT SURVIVED UNTIL THE 1890S WHEN IT WAS REBUILT FROM THE GROUND UP. WHILE IT RETAINS ITS EARLIER FORM, MANY DETAILS, INCLUD-ING, PERHAPS, THE ISLAMIC TOUCHES, REVEAL TURN-OF-THE-CENTURY TASTES. *Page 59, detail:* A DETAIL OF AN EARLY SIXTEENTH-CENTURY MOSAIC FROM A SYNAGOGUE IN ISFAHAN, IRAN, SHOWS ARABIC INFLUENCE. *Above:* THE SMALL AVRAHAM TOLEDANO SYNAGOGUE, BUILT AROUND 1790, IS ONE OF MANY PRIVATE FAMILY SYNAGOGUES ALONG THE CALLE DES SYNAGOGUES IN TANGIERS, MOROCCO. ONE ENTERS THROUGH A SMALL VESTIBULE, DESCENDS THREE STEPS INTO A SMALL, ENCLOSED, SKYLIGHTED COURTYARD, AND THEN HEADS INTO A TWO-STORY SANCTUARY SPACE WITHIN A SERIES OF ARCHES CARRIED ON COLUMNS. THE SYNAGOGUE IS FILLED WITH HANGING OIL LAMPS THAT ARE TYPICAL OF MOROCCO AND ARE ALSO VISIBLE IN MANUSCRIPT ILLUSTRATIONS OF SPANISH MEDIEVAL SYNAGOGUES. *Opposite:* TANGIERS' ASSAYAG SYNAGOGUE, BUILT IN 1840, IS INVISIBLE FROM THE STREET. ONE ENTERS THROUGH A SERIES OF VESTIBULES. THE SANCTUARY CONSISTS OF A NARROW TWO-STORY NAVE FLANKED BY ONE-STORY AISLES. ABOVE ONE OF THE AISLES AND THE REAR IS A MEZZANINE; ON THE THIRD SIDE, A LARGE WALL OF WINDOWS FLOODS THE SYNAGOGUE WITH LIGHT.

The twelfth-century Spanish traveler Benjamin of Tudela reported large numbers of synagogues in many Muslim cities, including twenty-eight in Baghdad (this number had shrunk by 1951, when most Jews left the newly independent Iraq).

Archaeological finds in Egypt and Syria and Talmudic references to such structures as the great synagogue of Alexandria testify to the antiquity of Jewish traditions in these lands. The rise of Islam did not disrupt these traditions, though many edicts and actions by

Muslim rulers resulted in repression and popular violence against Jews, destroying property, including synagogues. Under most Muslim regimes, however, the Jewish culture was tolerated, and the practice of Judaism allowed.

As in medieval Europe, many synagogues were privately founded in homes—often on the upper floors of multifamily dwellings. Examples of these synagogues can still be seen throughout the *mellah*s, Jewish quarters, of Morocco. Embedded within the residential fabric, they served the worship needs of extended families and were protected from scrutiny or vandalism from without.

Height restrictions kept roofs low but encouraged builders to lower floors to allow spacious interiors. Exteriors were nondescript, usually without identifying markers. Whenever possible, synagogues had courtyards, which served a multitude of ritual and social purposes and usually contained a water source. The courtyard also allowed the ornamentation of a secondary facade, which led directly into the prayer hall. Synagogues were often richly decorated within, adorned with painted patterns, tilework, stucco, and fine woodwork. Many synagogues were lavishly covered with floor and wall rugs, and congregants were expected to remove shoes upon entering. The multitude of hanging oil lamps of glass, brass, and other metals found in these synagogues is particularly striking. Such lamps were functional, but also served a commemorative purpose.

There is no established synagogue plan type from the Arab world, but variants of the basilica were popular throughout the Jewish community from the Middle Ages until the twentieth century. The antiquity of the design and its similarity to the multi-aisle mosque plan probably account for its popularity. One

of the oldest synagogues known, the Ben Ezra (founded 882, in Cairo), was of this type.

From the late fifteenth century, when refugees from Spain started to settle in the Muslim world, particularly within the extensive boundaries of the Ottoman Empire, Sephardic traditions began to influence and eventually dominate synagogue design and decoration throughout the lands around the Mediterranean; this can be seen today especially in the architecture of Morocco and Syria.

In Morocco, there is continuity of design in Sephardic synagogues with those of Spain. For example, the Fessaine Synagogue in Fez recalls the plans of synagogues from Toledo and Segovia. In Syria, the basilica form was popular during the Ottoman period. Syrian synagogue interiors frequently comprise a wider central aisle and two side aisles, separated by arcades carried by columns or piers. Sometimes, sections of the central aisles are raised to better illuminate the interior, especially the tevah. The resulting "lightbox" is functional, since light is needed to read the Torah, but it also symbolic.

TEVOT AND HECHALOT

Most synagogues in Muslim lands have readers' platforms near their centers. A remarkable feature of Syrian synagogues is the large, ornate tevah. Most Syrian *tevot* (plural of tevah) are octagonal and reached by four steps. Slender wood columns rise from the octagon corners to support an open canopylike covering, always of painted wood. Upon entering, one sees the tevah, from where God's law is proclaimed, set apart in a square of natural light. Additional lighting comes from clerestory windows or windows

Opposite: VISITING THE AL-GHRIBA SYNAGOGUE IS A SENSUAL AS WELL AS A SPIRITUAL EXPERIENCE. THE RICH COLORS—REDS, BLUES, AND GOLD—AND THE MIX OF MATERIALS—STONE, WOOD, AND CLOTH—ALL COMBINE TO CREATE AN ALMOST OTHERWORLDLY SANCTUARY FROM THE EVERYDAY WORLD OF DJERBA, TUNISIA. *Above:* LIKE MOST OF THE DAMSCENE SYNAGOGUES BUILT DURING THE OTTOMAN PERIOD, THE RACQY SYNAGOGUE OF DAMASCUS IS A BASILICA WITH A PROMINENT TEVAH IN ITS CENTRAL AISLE.

in the walls of the side aisles, as well as from hanging oil lamps.

Throughout the Muslim world it was common to find multiple arks within synagogues or arks flanked by niches for prayer books or ritual objects. It was not unusual for synagogues to possess large numbers of Torah scrolls, often written to commemorate important members of the community. The Great Synagogue in Baghdad is said to have had over seventy Torahs.

Most Syrian *hechalot* (plural of hechal) consist of double niches, enclosed by ornately carved wood doors, approached by three stairs. The hechalot are draped with ornamental curtains, and many are still filled with Torah scrolls,

kept in cases that stand on end and open like a book, revealing the scroll within. The Torah is read in its case (called a *tik*), set vertically. These cases are the most ornately worked religious items within the Syrian synagogues.

In many synagogues, congregants sat on carpeted floors. More often, benches encircled the interiors. These were either built into the walls (as at the Great Synagogue of Aleppo) or against them. Benches were also set around the tevah and frequently under the arches of aisle arcades.

Synagogues usually served men only. Women could congregate outside the windows and doors, as is still the case in Casablanca.

Above: The Great Synagogue of Aleppo is really two synagogues built together. The earlier consists of an open court for outdoor services, and an enclosed basilica was built next to it. This vaulted aisle runs between the two and leads directly to a hechal known as the "cave of Elijah," where valuable books and scrolls used to be stored. *Opposite:* The seventeenth-century Rabbi Shlomo ibn Danan Synagogue in Fez was built and owned for generations by one of the most prominent Jewish Moroccan families. The interior is a notably high room of two naves divided by octagonal piers. Remarkably, though the synagogue has been abandoned for decades, all of its original furnishings remain. These, together with the building itself, are now being restored.

THE OLD SYNAGOGUE OF ALEPPO

ONE OF THE OLDEST and most venerated synagogues in the Muslim world is the Old Synagogue of Aleppo, a sanctuary with traditional associations dating back to the Prophet Elijah. The connection is not impossible, as Aleppo is the oldest continuously occupied city in the world, and Jews have lived in Syria for millennia.

The synagogue was built in the Byzantine period, perhaps as early as the ninth century. After being damaged in the Mongol sack of Aleppo in 1400, it underwent extensive changes in 1405–18, and with the arrival of Spanish exiles in Aleppo during the sixteenth century, a new wing on the eastern side of the main courtyard was built. At the end of the western aisle of this wing, on the southern part facing Jerusalem, is the hechal, known as the "cave of Elijah." It was in this ark that the *Keter Aram Tzova* (Aleppo Codex), the earliest known manuscript of the complete Bible, was kept.

In the central courtyard stood a raised, roofed reader's platform. The congregation sat around a spacious courtyard in porticoes while the main ark was placed in a niche in the wall. The synagogue remained essentially unchanged until it was looted, burned, and heavily damaged in the anti-Jewish riots of 1947. It was partially rebuilt in the 1980s but there are now no Jews in Aleppo to use it, and it remains silent and empty.

THE RABBI SHLOMO IBN DANAN SYNAGOGUE

IN FEZ, MOROCCO, probably roughly contemporary with the Fessaine Synagogue, is the Rabbi Shlomo ibn Danan Synagogue. This was the private synagogue of the Danan family and their supporters, recalling the Spanish HaLevi Synagogue in Toledo, though its form is distinct.

One enters from a small street widening through an unimpressive door into a small vestibule, and then, turning, heads into a wide and tall well-lit space, a revelation after the tight-knit street network of the surrounding mellah. The hechal fills one wall—it is a series of recessed cabinets with finely made wooden doors, surrounded by an

Mud Synagogues

In many parts of Morocco and in Yemen, remnants of synagogues can be found in small villages where the build-ings are all of traditional mud con-struction. Synagogues in these centers are simple in design but often impres-sive in the types of spaces they create.

In Morocco, a common type features aisles surrounding a central open space in which were placed the wooden tevah and hechal on dried mud supports. In these buildings, standard architectural elements, such as the square pier and the pointed arch, are fully articulated in the mud, which when dry, hardens to a stonelike consistency. When not maintained, however, these buildings quickly deteriorate, and today they sur-vive only as ruins.

Opposite: A DISTINCTIVE FEATURE OF THE AL-GHRIBA SYNAGOGUE AND MANY OTHER NORTH AFRICAN SYNAGOGUES IS THEIR APPARENT INFORMALITY. WORSHIPERS COME TO STUDY AND PRAY AT ALL TIMES OF DAY AND FEEL AT HOME IN THE SANCTUARY SPACE. *Above:* THE COURTYARD OF THE AL-GHRIBA SYNAGOGUE IS UNIMPOSING AND DOES NOT PREPARE THE VISITOR FOR THE RICH COLORS WITHIN. THE SPACE PLAYS AN IMPORTANT PART IN THE FESTIVAL CELEBRATIONS OF THE THOUSANDS OF PILGRIMS WHO VISIT THE SYNAGOGUE EVERY YEAR.

ornate carved and painted stucco frame. There are colored tiles on the walls, and the room is filled with wooden benches and chairs, many painted or inlaid with elaborate designs. Across from the hechal is the tevah, a raised platform confined behind an arched wooden screen. The actual table on which the Torah scroll is set is narrow, and it is surmounted by an ornate gilded-metal openwork canopy.

THE AL-GHRIBA SYNAGOGUE ON DJERBA

THE AL-GHRIBA SYNAGOGUE on the Tunisian island of Djerba, with its blue walls, is one of the best examples of an adaptable space, where the behavior of the congregant or visitor is not rigorously programmed, typical of synagogues in Muslim lands.

Legend has it that the synagogue was founded by refugees who, following the destruction of Solomon's Temple, brought one of the Temple gates to Djerba, where it is reputedly encased within the synagogue walls. While there seems to be no basis for this, the synagogue is indeed old and has been venerated for generations, though it probably actually dates to the Middle Ages. It has been particularly favored as a pilgrimage site for Jews from all

over North Africa, who come especially on the holiday of Lag ba-Omer.

IN THE HOLY LAND

UNDER TURKISH RULE, a number of domed synagogues were built throughout North Africa and the Middle East, including several in Jerusalem (Hurva, Tiferet Israel, Prophet Elijah, and Istanbul synagogues), which clearly show the influence of contemporary mosque design. The domed Abraham Avninu Synagogue of Hebron was built in the fifteenth century but destroyed in 1929.

Synagogues proliferated in other cities in what is now Israel during the period of Turkish rule. Excepting Jerusalem, no place had more synagogues than Safed, which became a center of Jewish mysticism in the sixteenth century, at the end of which there were thirty-two synagogues in the city, with plans to build more. Many of these are still in use. The most renowned of these were the two synagogues named after the famous kabbalist Isaac Luria HaAri. One of these was Sephardic and is closely related to the synagogues of Damascus, with a single nave with three hechalot on the south wall, and a large freestanding tevah dominating the center.

CENTERS OF JEWISH LIFE

THE SYNAGOGUES of Muslim lands reflect a wide range of historical circumstances and local cultural influences. All served as foci of their communities—the centerpieces of Jewish identity within a non-Jewish world. Today only a small number of these diverse structures survive, and few even of these are utilized. They remain, however, powerful reminders of a once rich and varied Jewish life, a golden age, under Muslim rule.

Opposite: The Hurva Synagogue in Jerusalem, also called Beth Yaacov after Baron James Rothschild, who provided funds for its completion in 1705, was destroyed in 1721—hence, its common name, which means "ruin." A new synagogue designed by Assad Bey and funded by philanthropist Moses Montefiore was built on the site from 1856 to 1864 and served as a center of Jewish life in Palestine until it was destroyed in 1948. A single arch has been restored in the synagogue which is again a ruin—now left that way by choice. *Above:* Roughly contemporary with the Hurva Synagogue, the El Franj in Damascus remains intact and in use by the small Jewish community still in that city. The synagogue is a basilica with limestone columns supporting stone arches, which shelter finely wrought and richly colored furnishings and fittings.

Above: The small Rabbi Baba Salili Synagogue in Erfoud, Morocco, was probably built in the 1920s. It features traditional Moroccan architectural elements such as horseshoe arches and octagonal columns. While no longer used for worship, the building is now cared for by the Moroccan family that has adapted it for use as a home. One can still see the hechal set into the east wall. *Opposite:* Like many private Moroccan synagogues, the Rabbi Mamoun Synagogue in Fez was located within a residential building. Stairs led to an area set aside for women, separate from the main prayer space.

UNEXPECTED WORLDS

Synagogues in India and East Asia

❧

JEWISH COMMUNITIES ALSO FLOURISHED
beyond the borders of Christian and Muslim lands.
These communities–in India, China, and elsewhere
in Asia–while centuries, even millennia old, have only
recently received attention from Western visitors
and scholars, and much remains to be learned of their
legend-shrouded histories. In many places, especially in
India, fine synagogues remain, a few still in use.

Pages 72-73: AN INSCRIPTION DATES THE ORIGINAL SYNAGOGUE AT PARUR, INDIA, TO 1164. THE PRESENT SYNAGOGUE, WHICH IS NO LONGER USED, WAS ERECTED ON THE SITE BY DAVID YAACOB KASTIEL IN EITHER 1586 OR 1616. A HEBREW POEM INSCRIBED ON THE EAST WALL DECLARES "HE WHO DWELT IN ROCK AND BUSH/MAY HE DWELL FOR HIS SAKE IN MY HOUSE [SYNAGOGUE]." Page 73, detail: THIS CLOSE-UP SHOWS ONE OF THE HUNDREDS OF BLUE-AND-WHITE WILLOW-PATTERNED CHINESE TILES DATING FROM THE EIGHTEENTH CENTURY THAT COVER THE FLOOR OF THE PARADESI SYNAGOGUE IN COCHIN, INDIA. Above: THE INTERIOR WHITE WALLS OF THE PARADESI SYNAGOGUE CONTRAST WITH A RICH ARRAY OF BELGIAN CRYSTAL CHANDELIERS AND LANTERNS. A CURVED BRASS CENTRAL BIMAH, WOOD BENCHES, AND THE HUNDREDS OF FLOOR TILES CREATE A DAZZLING YET SERENE WORSHIP SPACE. Opposite: THE PARADESI SYNAGOGUE SITS WITHIN A LARGE COMPLEX OF RELATED BUILDINGS AND OPEN SPACES SITUATED AT THE END OF SYNAGOGUE LANE, ADJACENT TO THE MAHARAJAH'S PALACE AND NOT FAR FROM THE DOCKS OF COCHIN.

THE JEWS OF COCHIN

THE LARGEST GROUP of Indian synagogues is found in the state of Kerala, on the southwest coast of India. For centuries, the Kerala Jewish community has been centered in the villages around Cochin. The Jews of Cochin could not have survived had it not been for the protection and liberty afforded them by the rajah of Cochin.

The origin of the Jewish association with Cochin and the Malabar coast is obscure, but the earliest evidence of Jewish settlement in Cochin is given by two copper plates, now preserved at the Paradesi Synagogue, which most scholars date to between 974 and 1020 C.E., though local legend places them around the fourth century C.E. Benjamin of Tudela, the Spanish Jewish traveler, indicated that there were about a thousand Jews in the region around the year 1170, and that they were black like their neighbors and meticulously observed the Torah, but his account is controversial.

Two waves of immigration converged on Cochin in the early sixteenth century. First,

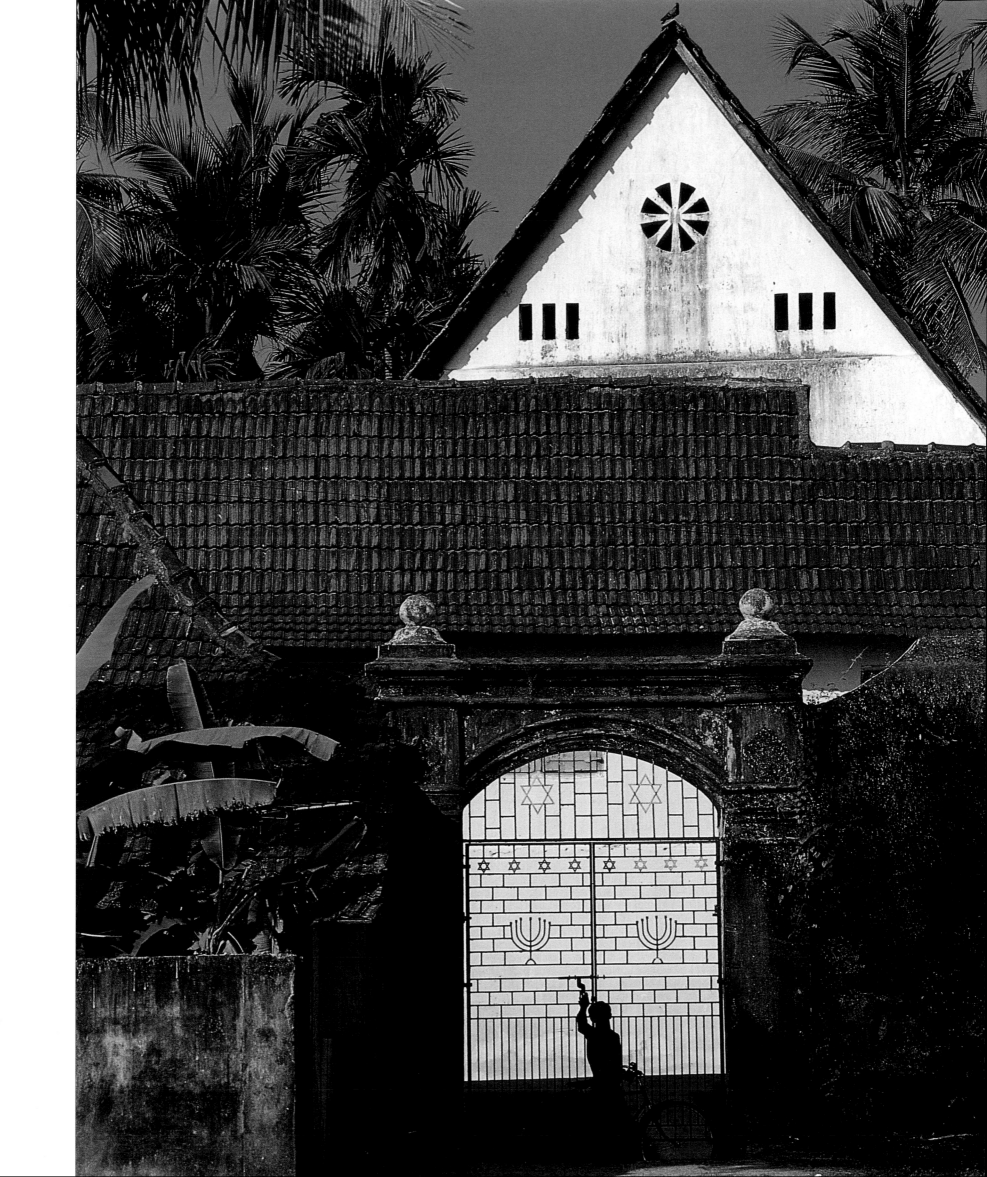

there were Jews who came from Cranganore (Shinkali, Shingly), the original Jewish settlement on the Malabar coast, after the destruction by the Portuguese around 1524. Second was the arrival of Jews and New Christians (Jews forcibly converted to Christianity) from Spain and Portugal. Jews had been expelled from Spain in 1492 and from Portugal in 1497. Some Sephardic Jews came via Turkey and Syria, arriving in Cochin in 1511. A Jewish traveler who came from Yemen, Zechariah al-Dahiri (c. 1550), says that he "met with many Jews in Cushi [Cochin]," where he had stayed for three months.

Granted land next to the rajah's palace in Mattancheri, the Jews developed a quarter that came to be known as Jew Town, which was centered upon one long north-south street called "Synagogue Lane." Between the sixteenth and seventeenth centuries, the Jews of Kerala had about nine synagogues. Jews built two synagogues in Mattancheri and named them after two of the synagogues left behind in Shingly. The Kadavumbhagam, built in 1539, is located a quarter mile (.4 km) south of the rajah's palace. The unusual octagonal structure is now a warehouse. The interior furnishings of the synagogue were dismantled and shipped to Israel in 1991.

The Paradesi Synagogue

The Paradesi Synagogue was built by descendants of Spanish, Dutch, and other European Jews in 1568. The building, a simple square with a gabled roof of ceramic tile supporting an open cupola with a wide-eaved cap, is preceded by a Dutch-style clock tower, built in 1761. The numerals on the clock facing the synagogue are in Hebrew, the one facing Synagogue Lane is in Roman numerals, and the one facing the harbor is in Malayalam, the local language.

Passing through the external door on the southeastern side of the building, one enters a small anteroom. To the left, a stairway leads to the women's section, and directly ahead a second doorway leads into the courtyard and the entrance to the synagogue proper. The walls of the synagogue are thick, and each shuttered window has a wide, comfortable window seat before it.

The architecture of the interior is quite simple, with white plaster walls creating a neutral backdrop to the rich decoration. Hundreds of blue-and-white willow-patterned Chinese tiles, brought to Cochin in 1762, cover the floor. A curved all-brass bimah is in the center of the room. Silver and brass chandeliers and oil lamps hang from the carved wood ceiling. The intricate teak ark, painted gold with red decoration, is a fine example of Kerala wood carving. At the north side of the ark is the beautifully carved chair of Elijah, used in circumcision ceremonies.

The upper-level women's section of the synagogue is set back from, rather than overlooking, the downstairs space. A latticework divider, placed in front of the section, separates the women from an unusual synagogue

feature, a second bimah, situated above the rear quarter of the male-occupied sanctuary. This bimah is approached by a small stairway in the corner of the sanctuary. From here, the Torah is read on the Sabbath and festival days, and important prayers are recited during daily services. The lower bimah is used for everyday prayers in the morning, afternoon, and evening.

Above: NOT FAR FROM COCHIN IS THE SYNAGOGUE AT CHENDAMANGALAM, BUILT IN 1420 AND REBUILT IN 1614. ABOVE THE SYNAGOGUE ENTRANCE IS A PAINTED WOOD RELIEF REPRESENTING THE MENORAH AND OLIVE TREES DESCRIBED IN THE PROPHET ZECHARIAH'S VISION OF A MENORAH. INSIDE THE UNUSED SANCTUARY IS MORE EXCEPTIONAL WOODWORK—AN ARK THAT IS DECAYING IN THE TROPICAL HEAT. *Opposite:* THE MUSMEAH YESHUA (HEBREW "BRINGS FORTH SALVATION") SYNAGOGUE IN RANGOON, BURMA, BUILT IN 1893, IS ONE OF SEVERAL BRITISH-ERA SYNAGOGUES IN EAST ASIA. WALKING DOWN A NARROW STREET AND PASSING THROUGH HIGH WHITE WALLS, ONE ENTERS THE SANCTUARY—A JEWISH REFUGE (NOW HARDLY USED) IN THIS MUSLIM AND BUDDHIST LAND.

CHINA

PERHAPS THE MOST unexpected synagogue in the world is the one that existed in Kaifeng, China, where Jews active in the silk route had settled in the Middle Ages. The community's first synagogue was apparently built in 1163 and was eventually surrounded by other structures. It was destroyed in a flood in 1461. A replacement was burned around 1600, and the final synagogue was dedicated in 1663. It occupied a large lot and over time was surrounded by a wide range of ancillary buildings–a study hall, a mikvah, a communal kitchen, and a kosher butcher.

Based on early-eighteenth-century drawings by the Jesuit missionary Jean Domenge, we know that the building was pagodalike, with a three-tiered roof. Statues of lions flanked the entrance, from which one passed through the East Gate, a memorial gate, and then the Great Gateway of the first courtyard. A similar progression led through two more courtyards, until one entered the sanctuary. Wooden lacquered pillars divided the space into a central nave flanked by two side aisles. According to Domenge, the interior contained a ceremonial table with censer, flower vases, candlesticks, and oil bowls (ceremonial objects found in Chinese temples). Beyond this was a "throne of Moses" (a bimah), and farther, a canopy-covered table where the emperor's tablet was displayed; then, at the far end, was the "ark of the Revered Scriptures," which contained thirteen Torah scrolls in individual cases. The Kaifeng Jewish community declined so that by

the mid-nineteenth century there were no Jews who could read Hebrew or maintain the synagogue, which was demolished around 1860.

Also in the nineteenth century, Ashkenazi Jews from eastern Europe moved across Asia and settled in Shanghai, expanding the Jewish presence established in the 1840s by Sephardic merchants. The Ohel Moishe Synagogue was built in Shanghai in 1907 by Russian Jews first fleeing persecution and massacres in Tsarist Russia and in eastern Europe, and then, after 1917, fleeing the Russian Revolution. The populations of these communities were augmented by Jewish refugees from Europe during the Nazi period, so that on the eve of World War II there were ten thousand Jews in Shanghai.

In the prewar period there were seven synagogues in Shanghai, including the large domed Beth Aaron Synagogue on Museum Road built in 1927 in a neo-Byzantine style similar to many contemporary synagogues in the United States. The last Shanghai synagogue (the New Synagogue in the French Concession) was erected in 1941. Jews also settled in Harbin, where a large synagogue combining Moorish and central Asian architectural motifs was built in 1907.

THE JEWS OF ASIA

IN OTHER PARTS OF ASIA, however, particularly in centers of maritime trade, new Jewish communities were established in the nineteenth century. These communities were led by families of Sephardic Jews with connections to the Egyptian, Iraqi, and Indian Jewish communities, who found protection and prosperity in Hong Kong, Shanghai, Rangoon, and Singapore under British colonial rule. Impressive synagogues, similar in expression to the Iraqi synagogues in Calcutta and Bombay, are still in use in all these locales.

Jacob Sassoon sponsored the erection of Hong Kong's Ohel Leah Synagogue (named after his mother), built in 1901 by the local architectural firm of Leigh and Orange in the Hong Kong Midlevels, after he had moved there from Shanghai. Until recently, the white synagogue, with its short twin octagonal towers flanking a projecting Palladian porch, was a stately beacon visible far out at sea. Though saved from demolition in the late 1980s, it is now hemmed in by skyscrapers.

Not to be outdone by Hong Kong, the Jews of Singapore, led by Menasseh Meyer, built the impressive Oxley Rise Synagogue in 1900–06, after designs by architect R.A.J. Bidwell. Like the Sassoons, Meyer came from Iraq, and the elaborate eclectic Italianate architecture of Oxley Rise recalls the Ezra Synagogue in Calcutta and Hong Kong's Ohel Leah. The large basilica is noteworthy for its exterior porticoes over which are set the interior women's galleries, leaving three full-height aisles within for the congregation's men.

With the exception of the oldest synagogues of Cochin, and the long-lost synagogue of Kaifeng, there is no indigenous synagogue-building tradition in the Asian subcontinent or in East Asia. In the nineteenth and twentieth centuries the Jewish communities in these regions were closely tied to colonial powers— primarily the British—and their architecture derives from trends in Europe. With the exception of painting their synagogues a brilliant white in keeping with much of the British colonial architecture in Asia, and in providing generous windows and porticoes, the relatively staid Victorian and Edwardian designs owe little to their exotic locations.

7

GLORY

Emancipation

and Reform

MANY HAVE CALLED THE NINETEENTH CENTURY
the age of "cathedral synagogues." Clearly the builders
of synagogues were consciously competing with their
Christian neighbors in a quest for legitimacy. Local governments
or national rulers often encouraged this architectural
exhibitionism as a valid replacement of the historic squalor of
Jewish quarters and as an incentive to draw Jews into
the emerging mainstream national cultures.

EMANCIPATION OF THE JEWS

THE AGE OF EMANCIPATION of the Jews in Europe began after the French Revolution, during Napoleon's reign, when Jewish communities throughout the Napoleonic lands were reorganized into a system that mirrored the secular administration. This organization, along with the Jews' new legal and social status, had a profound impact on the location, appearance, and use of synagogues, as well as many other aspects of Jewish communal life.

For the first time in centuries, synagogue architecture was no longer a private affair of the Jewish community but a public enterprise guided, and sometimes controlled, by the city or state. Private synagogues were closed throughout France, and rabbis and other Jewish religious leaders were required to wear new clerical dress similar to their Christian counterparts. For state officials this was a way of elevating Judaism to a level of state recognition on par with Christian denominations. For many Jews, however, it amounted to a continuation of the long tradition dating back to Greek and Roman insistence that Jews conform to contemporary cultural and religious norms.

In the first part of the nineteenth century many synagogues were erected in the prevalent neoclassical style. In France, the new Jewish organization erected the Temple of the Rue Notre-Dame-de-Nazareth in 1822 as a basilica with a restrained Doric articulation. Although the synagogue actually followed the newly dominant Ashkenazic rite, its architecture reflected the traditional Sephardic nature of the French community, utilizing a bipolar plan with seats along the sides. But a pulpit set along the side is unusual and shows the influence of contemporary Catholic Church arrangements.

Pages 80-81: THE LEADERS OF THE NINETEENTH-CENTURY FRENCH JEWISH COMMUNITY, UNDER CLOSE SUPERVISION BY GOVERNMENT AUTHORITIES, CHOSE AN IMPOSING ROMANESQUE STYLE FOR THE MAIN SYNAGOGUE OF FRANCE. BUILT IN PARIS FROM 1861 TO 1874 ON THE RUE DE LA VICTOIRE AND DESIGNED BY ALFRED PHILIBERT ALDROPHE, IT REMAINS AMONG THE GRANDEST SYNAGOGUES IN EUROPE. *Page 81, detail:* THIS LEADED GLASS WINDOW SITS JUST UNDER THE DOME OF THE SYNAGOGUE IN GYOR, HUNGARY. *Above:* HUNDREDS OF "CATHEDRAL SYNAGOGUES" ON THE SCALE OF THIS ONE IN HANOVER, GERMANY, BUILT FROM 1862 TO 1870 IN THE GERMAN RENAISSANCE STYLE BY JEWISH ARCHITECT EDWIN OPPLER, WERE ERECTED ACROSS EUROPE IN THE SECOND HALF OF THE NINETEENTH CENTURY. THE MAJORITY OF THESE, LIKE THIS BUILDING, WERE DESTROYED BETWEEN 1938 AND 1945. *Opposite:* THE TEMPIO ISRAELITICO, DEDICATED IN 1882 IN FLORENCE, ITALY, COMBINES RENAISSANCE GEOMETRIES AND MASSING WITH MOORISH DETAILING TO CREATE AN ITALIAN VERSION OF THE POPULAR "CATHEDRAL SYNAGOGUE."

Thus, assimilated Polish Jews, builders of the Tempel Synagogue in Cracow and the Tlomakie Street Synagogue in Warsaw, became "Poles of the Mosaic Faith." In Italy, Jews were now recognized as Italians belonging to the "Israelite Community." Their architectural creations, such as the so-called "Mole Antoniana" in Turin, the Tempio Israelitico in Rome, and the Great Synagogue in Florence, are witness to this proud—if perhaps misguided—profession of Jewish involvement in contemporary society.

Assimilationist trends in Germany were succinctly summarized by German Jewish architect Edwin Oppler: "A German Jew living in a German state should build in a German style."

THE REFORM MOVEMENT

I⊤ WAS IN THE CONTEXT OF emancipation that the Jewish Reform movement developed in Germany at the beginning of the nineteenth century, gradually evolving into different forms and reaching countries farther east—notably Poland and Hungary—by mid-century.

Like the French Revolution itself, the Jewish Reform movement had roots in the French Enlightenment. Skepticism about traditional Jewish beliefs was now coupled on the part of many influential Jews with apprehension and embarrassment about Jewish community organization and the outward appearance of Jews in general. A move toward greater decorum and conformity was encouraged as a way of furthering Jewish assimilation into the new national cultures.

Israel Jacobson, a Jewish merchant from Halberstadt, Germany, played an important role in this process when he founded, in 1801, an industrial school at Seesen (in Brunswick) for both Jewish and Christian young men. He later built for the students of this school what he called a "Temple," dedicated on July 17, 1810, with over forty clergymen of "both religions" in attendance. In his inaugural address, Jacobson made reference to the Temple of Solomon, of which he said his own small temple was but a "humble copy." This was the first Reform Temple.

Opposite and above: A NEW SYNAGOGUE WAS BUILT IN ROME, ITALY, IN 1901-04, AFTER MUCH OF THE GHETTO AREA, INCLUDING THE VENERATED "CINQUE SCUOLE" (FIVE SYNAGOGUES), WAS DEMOLISHED DURING THE BUILDING OF EMBANKMENTS FOR THE TIBER RIVER. THE NEW SYNAGOGUE, WITH ITS DISTINCTIVE SQUARE-BASED DOME, RIVALED ST. PETER'S ON THE ROME SKYLINE. THE INTERIOR, DESIGNED BY COSTA & ARMANNI, RECALLS CONTEMPORARY SETS FOR VERDI OPERAS.

Efforts to harmonize traditional Judaism with common usage were reflected in the synagogue's interior. A pulpit stood in front of the ark, from which sermons were preached. The desk for the reader stood below. Both pulpit and reader's desk were enclosed by a canopied tabernacle supported by eight columns. Seen for the first time was a reader's desk with the preacher's pulpit placed a few steps above it, both in the area of the ark.

This conflation of traditional synagogue elements into a single architectural ensemble at the front of the sanctuary revolutionized the appearance and activity of the synagogue. The new interior arrangement promoted separation of leader and congregation, and created a new dynamic, already known in churches, between performer and audience. Increasingly, Reform leaders would exhort congregations to behave with regularity and unity in prayer, and the reorganization of the service by Reform rabbis created this new relation between *hazan* (cantor) and congregation. The congregation members became more passive observers of prayer and performance, signifying assent and approval through collective response.

Architecturally, the new Reform arrangement, which subsequently was adapted by many Modern Orthodox congregations, reduced the dynamic force of the synagogue service, where separation of bimah and ark had always produced a ritual tension between sacred spaces.

ROMANESQUE AND MOORISH SYNAGOGUES

THE LARGE SYNAGOGUES built throughout Europe from the late 1830s onward were sometimes built for reasons other than to accommodate a rising population. When synagogues were planned, advocates argued that existing buildings were overcrowded on major holidays. Opponents, who usually lost the arguments, wanted to solve the problem by hiring halls to accommodate the overflow. Knowing that assimilation in general culture

and in architecture often was related, they worried about the spiritual danger of imitating the practice of building large churches. Proponents of building usually won out, and Europe was dotted with enormous urban synagogues hardly distinguishable in size, and often in design, from contemporary churches.

These impressive, costly (and often half-empty) structures were built in a variety of architectural styles, in keeping with general nineteenth-century architectural trends, which favored historicism but allowed the coexistence of a multitude of historical styles. The style chosen for the exterior decoration of a struc-

ture could send meaningful messages to Jews and non-Jews alike. Especially popular styles for synagogues were the Romanesque and the so-called Moorish styles. Variants of the Gothic style, with its pointed arches, pinnacles, and elaborate tracery, were less common because of their more immediate association with late medieval church architecture.

The Romanesque style provided an image for synagogues that suited Jews as well as Christians. Most Jews did not want to be mistaken for Christians, but they wanted equal rights and opportunities. They wanted their religion–and hence their synagogues—to be recognized as distinct yet still belonging to the modern world of nationalism and enlightenment. The Romanesque style seemed to offer this. It had historical connections for Jews, linking new buildings, such as the scores of synagogues erected in French Alsace, with the medieval synagogue at Worms, and it could also be adapted to reflect regional styles.

The building that effectively made use of the Romanesque style and introduced a more ornate and exotic alternative was the synagogue of Dresden, designed by the prominent architect Gottfried Semper and built in 1838–40. The exterior was in a serious, yet sedate, Romanesque style, but inside Semper employed a rich combination of decorative forms inspired by medieval Spanish sources, especially the Islamic decorations from the Alhambra at Granada. While this was hardly a Jewish provenance, it wasn't Christian in

Above and opposite: THE DOHANY STREET SYNA-GOGUE, IN BUDAPEST, HUNGARY, IS EUROPE'S LARGEST JEWISH WORSHIP SPACE. ITS TWO-TOWERED FACADE WAS WIDELY IMITATED THROUGHOUT THE AUSTRO-HUNGARIAN EMPIRE; EVEN TODAY, MINIATURE VERSIONS CAN BE FOUND IN TOWNS IN AT LEAST SIX CENTRAL EUROPEAN COUNTRIES.

origin. Better yet, it recalled the "Golden Age" of Jews under Islamic Spanish rule.

Semper's attempt to identify and create a new Jewish style resonated, and over the next half century this new Spanish, or "Moorish," style became increasingly prominent in synagogue design and decoration, quickly migrating from the interior, as at Dresden, to the exterior of synagogues in Vienna, Budapest, Berlin, Zagreb, and elsewhere. By the late nineteenth century the Moorish style was widely recognized as a Jewish style.

Two other buildings, erected within a few decades, especially influenced Jewish architectural taste and synagogue design. In one of the earliest public displays of community confidence and identity, Vienna's Jews erected the Templegasse Synagogue, designed by Ludwig von Forster, between 1853 and 1858. Von Forster adopted Semper's Moorish decoration but lavishly applied it to the exterior of the synagogue as well. The effect was a frothy Viennese pastry but with an "Oriental" flavor. The large galleried interior continued the ostentatious display. The building communicated a message of Jewish exoticism but also possessed a religious and cultural vibrancy as part of the new multicultural society.

In Budapest, the Jewish congregation, which dated to the Middle Ages, engaged von Forster to design an even bigger building–the Dohany Street Synagogue–now the largest synagogue in use in Europe. More austere on the outside than its Viennese counterpart, the building's exterior architecture suggests stability and confidence. The large brick arches of the entrance recall traditional Romanesque motifs, but the patterned tiles have Moorish designs. The twin towers, prominent on the skyline of the city, announce the Jewish presence, but their unusual cupolas topped with copper balls surmounted by Jewish stars confidently pronounce Jewish

"otherness," too. Inside, the synagogue, which follows Reform configuration, with bimah and ark combined in an lavish display at the end of a long processional opposite the entrance wall, has two levels of galleries and can seat three thousand people.

The design of the Templegasse and Dohany Street synagogues influenced scores of synagogues built over the next half century throughout the Austro-Hungarian empire. Miniature versions, or rather plain buildings decorated with only a few elements borrowed from the big-city prototypes, such as the towers, grace cities in Hungary, Slovakia, the Czech Republic, Romania, and the former Yugoslavia. Many of the buildings still survive, albeit in seriously damaged or altered condition.

In the United States, too, echoes of these synagogues can frequently be found. The Plum Street Synagogue in Cincinnati owes much to Vienna, and the exterior of the Central Synagogue in New York is copied from the Dohany.

THE ORANIEN-BURGERSTRASSE SYNAGOGUE

GERMAN JEWS, not to be outdone by their Austro-Hungarian neighbors, embarked on massive building programs of their own. The most significant was the erection of the Neue Synagogue in Berlin, known as the Oranienburgerstrasse Synagogue, after its location.

Built from 1859 to 1866 based on designs by Eduard Knoblauch, the building was famous for its size, opulence, and creative use of new materials and technology. Its fame far exceeded the Jewish realm, earning attention in both the architectural and popular press in many countries, including a full-page illustration in the *London News* at the time of its dedication.

Like the Dohany Street Synagogue, the Oranienburgerstrasse Synagogue was flanked by two towers topped by almost spherical cupolas. The slightly recessed entrance was defined by three arched doorways. Most remarkable, however, was the placement of a huge dome over the vestibule area. The dome was set there instead of over the sanctuary to be seen from the street. The sanctuary angled away from the street deep into the building lot. The entrance block was the only part of the synagogue to survive Kristallnacht and the Allied bombing of Berlin. The glass and gilded-metal dome, recently restored, remains a dominant feature of Berlin's skyline.

Most of the structure was built of brick, iron, and glass, with details formed by combining Gothic and Moorish patterns in the new materials. The interior walls were richly painted with stenciled patterns. Attenuated columns supported the gallery and roof, the slenderness and height allowing the interior to appear open and the vaults exceedingly lofty. Large skylights lit the hall, and the latest inventions for gas lighting and better ventilation were installed throughout. The exuberance, elegance, and prominence of the synagogue were fully echoed by the behavior and social standing of Berlin's mid-century Jewish community. The evening dress worn to the dedication by the congregants symbolized for many of Germany's nineteenth-century Jews their dignity, formality, and social status.

THE ORANIENBURGERSTRASSE SYNAGOGUE IN BERLIN, BUILT FROM 1859 TO 1866 BY ARCHITECT EDUARD KNOBLAUCH, WAS ONE OF THE MOST CELEBRATED BUILDINGS OF ITS TIME, RIVALING THE CRYSTAL PALACE IN ENGLAND. NOTED FOR ITS SIZE, ORNAMENT, AND MODERN MATERIALS, THIS SYNAGOGUE BECAME A NINETEENTH-CENTURY BERLIN ATTRACTION. TODAY, ITS PROMINENT FACADE WITH DOMES OF GLASS AND GILDED TRACERY HAS BEEN REBUILT, BUT THE MAIN SANCTUARY, DESTROYED DURING WORLD WAR II, HAS NOT BEEN REPLACED.

CONTEMPORARY DESIGNS

ALTERNATE DESIGNS for synagogues were numerous. Not everyone favored the new Moorish style—many felt it was too showy and historically inaccurate. One effective contemporary building was the synagogue in Gyor, Hungary, completed in 1866, the same year as the Oranienburgerstrasse Synagogue.

Designed by Benko Karoly, this square synagogue (no longer in use) has towers on its four corners and is topped by a high dome. The interior, however, is formed as an octagon, and seven sides were covered with two levels of galleries. The effect is like being inside a wedding cake that has been turned inside out. As at the Dohany Synagogue, freely interpreted Moorish motifs predominate, though in its strict geometry and fine proportions the synagogue also refers to Renaissance (church) designs.

In Germany, the impression made by the Oranienburgerstrasse Synagogue was strong, but few communities followed Berlin's lead. More common in German cities prior to the widespread destruction of 1938 were large, prominently located synagogues that employed a more traditional German architectural vocabulary—Romanesque, Gothic, or Renaissance. These synagogues, exemplified by the work of architect Edwin Oppler in Hamburg, Breslau (now Wroclaw, Poland), and elsewhere, really were cathedral synagogues, because they recalled so closely in scale, form, and decoration large Christian churches. Unlike in Vienna, Budapest, and Berlin, many of these synagogues were built on a cross plan. The east arm was usually reserved for the ark and bimah, the latter sometimes emerging farther into the central crossing area.

Like Oppler, Hungarian architect Lipot Baumhorn (1860–1932) also favored this plan. Baumhorn built or expanded twenty-eight synagogues throughout central Europe during his long career. Externally, these were in many styles, but formally they were of a type, and for Baumhorn this type kept getting bigger and bigger, culminating in his synagogue

Opposite: THE SYNAGOGUE AT SZEGED, HUNGARY, IS THE MASTERPIECE OF PROLIFIC SYNAGOGUE ARCHITECT LIPOT BAUMHORN, WHO WORKED CLOSELY WITH THE TOWN'S ESTEEMED RABBI IMMANUEL LOW ON THE DESIGN AND DECORATION. AN ENORMOUS DOME SURMOUNTS AN INTERIOR CONTAINING CHANDELIERS, MOSAICS, STAINED GLASS, AND A WALL ENTIRELY COVERED WITH ELABORATE DESIGNS. THE ARK WALL, LIKE THE BUILDING EXTERIOR, IS DESIGNED IN AN ORNATE GOTHIC STYLE. *Above:* THE ENORMOUS DOME OF THE SYNAGOGUE AT GYOR, HUNGARY, IS VISIBLE FOR MILES. THE UNUSUAL OCTAGONAL PLAN WITH CORNER TOWERS GIVES THE BUILDING A MASSIVE FORTIFIED APPEARANCE.

of Gyongyos, Hungary, completed in 1929. Among Baumhorn's most prized works is the synagogue of Szeged (1899-1903) in southern Hungary. The structure is a large Gothic pile, with an ornate cupola visible throughout much of the town. At Szeged, Baumhorn worked with the local rabbi, who was also a botanist, and together they decorated the synagogue with scores of images and reliefs of flowers and plants.

Baumhorn's design for Szeged was chosen in an open competition, something more and more Jewish communities were sponsoring. Competitions were still relatively new, and they encouraged many architects to try their hand at synagogue design. The second-place finisher in the Szeged competition was an exuberant design by Hungarian Jewish architects Komar and Iakab. Much more in tune with contemporary architectural trends, the design

incorporated local Hungarian folk motifs with a confident use of Art Nouveau or Secessionist curves and colors. The design was picked up by the town of Subotica, near Szeged, now just over the border in Yugoslavia. The Subotica synagogue was actually completed first, and the two comparably sized buildings—one heavily historic, the other excitingly new—represent the diversity of central European synagogue design at the turn of the century.

שאו ... שערים ראשיכם ... תהלים כ"ד

RECOVERY

Postwar
Synagogues

❦

Tʜᴇ ʟᴀɴᴅsᴄᴀᴘᴇ ᴏғ Jᴇᴡɪsʜ sᴇᴛᴛʟᴇᴍᴇɴᴛ
was completely transformed in the years following World War II.
Many of the oldest Jewish centers had been completely destroyed.
In these places, surviving Jews either moved on or faced the difficulties
of reconstituting what institutions they could and of rebuilding
synagogues or erecting entirely new structures. The focus of
Jewish building energy was largely transferred to
the newly established State of Israel.

Pages 92-93: IN THE NINETEENTH CENTURY, MANY SYNAGOGUES IN EUROPE AND NORTH AMERICA INTRODUCED STAINED GLASS WINDOWS, USUALLY FEATURING GEOMETRIC DESIGNS AND OCCASIONAL JEWISH SYMBOLS. THESE WINDOWS TENDED TO BE SELF-CONTAINED. IN THE POSTWAR PERIOD, WIDESPREAD USE OF NEW BUILDING MATERIALS ALLOWED THE CRE-ATION OF LARGE WINDOWS, OFTEN FILLING ENTIRE WALLS. CONTEMPORARY ARTISTS FREQUENTLY HAVE BEEN COMMISSIONED TO CREATE LARGE SWEEPING COMPOSITIONS IN COLORED GLASS, OF WHICH THIS DETAIL FROM JERUSALEM IS AN EXAMPLE. *Page 93, detail:* THIS STAINED GLASS WINDOW DECORATES TEMPLE EMANUEL IN PATTERSON, NEW JERSEY. *Above:* WHEN BUILT IN 1931, THE REFORM OBERSTRASSE SYNAGOGUE IN HAMBURG, GERMANY, PIONEERED MODERN BAUHAUS-INSPIRED DESIGN FOR RELIGIOUS BUILDINGS. THE SIMPLE GEOMETRY AND AUSTERE EXTERIOR OF THE BUILDING, DESIGNED BY FELIX ASCHER AND ROBERT FRIEDMANN, WAS INFLUENTIAL IN POSTWAR SYNAGOGUES IN EUROPE AND NORTH AMERICA. THE BUILDING IS NOW A RADIO STUDIO, BUT THE SIMPLE MENORAH RELIEF REMAINS OVER THE ENTRANCE.

Restoration was an option in some places, especially in countries like Italy and Hungary, where communities survived in their previous urban centers and synagogues had not been regularly targeted by the Nazis for destruction. In Germany, however, new synagogues were required for Jews who stayed, and the new German government was committed (or oblig-ed) to help construct them. Thus in Berlin and elsewhere new synagogues replaced the older ones, which, if they survived at all, were most-ly empty shells. Many of these ruins were sub-sequently demolished in the 1950s and 1960s.

For those Jews who did not stay in Europe, one destination was Palestine, soon to become the State of Israel. Here, in the first Jewish state in millennia, there was a need to build new syn-agogues. A few extant synagogues predated the 1930s but, overall, entirely new religious spaces had to be created. In the new Jewish state, the only limits synagogue architects faced were their imaginations and their budgets.

MODERNISM BEFORE THE WAR

IN EUROPE, NORTH AMERICA, and Israel, modern architecture was preferred for historic, aesthetic, and economic reasons. There had been previous experiments with modernism in synagogue design before the war. Indeed, it was in synagogues that the stripped-down modern style was first used for religious architecture. A few examples suffice to show the range of structures that prewar synagogue architects produced.

In Zilina, Slovakia, Peter Behrens of Berlin built a synagogue in 1928-30, which was, in many ways, a simplified version of the Byzantine domed synagogue popular in Hungary and the Balkans. Behrens's design set a half dome on a rectangular block, but within, the dome rises on slender concrete piers from a square, set within the rectangular mass. Outside, the ground floor is faced in stone, and the rest of the structure is made of reinforced concrete. Despite the use of concrete, the building looks traditional due to its massing and the monumental stairway that leads to the main entrance. Nothing about the building's architecture identifies it as a synagogue. Applied Stars of David set on each exterior corner serve this purpose.

In Amsterdam, architect A. Elzas built the International-style Lekstraat Synagogue in 1936-37. This building, a plain stone box with simple square windows, emphasizes only the ark and bimah. Elzas won a competition among nine Jewish architects for the commission, and even today the building ranks among the most sparely designed of synagogues. The simplicity of its geometry and white concrete walls is modified slightly by the stone on the exterior and the introduction of vast amounts of natural light through large windows.

In London, Sir Evan Owen Williams designed the modern Dollis Hill Synagogue (built 1933–34). The interior space is very open, as the galleries are cantilevered from the wall rather than supported by piers of columns. The walls and roof are made of a specially designed corrugated concrete that greatly strengthens the structure. Hexagonal and shield-shaped windows recall the Magen David, originally referred to as the Shield (not star) of David.

Above, top: BETH TZEDEC SYNAGOGUE IN TORONTO IS THE LARGEST IN CANADA, BUILT IN 1955 AFTER THE MERGER OF TWO CONGREGATIONS. ARCHITECT PETER DICKINSON'S MULTIFACETED DESIGN INCLUDES A MONUMENTAL BUT SEVERE INTERIOR FOCUSED UPON A MASSIVE BIMAH AND AN ARK, ARTICULATED WITH BRONZE DOORS SET BETWEEN GIANT SLABS OF MARBLE, CASCADING GOLD CURTAINS, AND BAS-RELIEFS BY ERNEST RABB, WHICH RISE THE FULL HEIGHT OF THE WALL AND DEPICT, ON ONE HUNDRED PANELS, TRADITIONAL JEWISH SYMBOLS. *Above, bottom:* THE SYNAGOGUE IN WISSEMBOURG, FRANCE, FEATURES A STARKLY MODERN FAÇADE.

SYNAGOGUES OF ISRAEL

Hundreds of synagogues were founded throughout Israel in the years just before and especially after independence, achieved in 1948. These were small structures, or rooms within structures, built and maintained by the diverse communities that came together to create the new state. Jews from Arab countries, eastern Europe, India, and elsewhere all tried to maintain their traditions, including the liturgy and organization of their synagogues. In some cases, as with the Italian Synagogue in Jerusalem, where interior elements of the synagogue from Conegliano Veneto, Italy, were installed in a preexisting building, communities literally attempted to recreate what they left behind. In the decades since, many of these have closed or combined, as second and third generations have intermarried and forged a new Israeli identity that often (but not always) supersedes previous group identification.

The modern style, which was simple to design, easy to replicate, and inexpensive to build, was preferred for synagogues. Israel was seen as modern and cut off from older European traditions. Jews were to be allowed to reinvent themselves, and architecture was one way of doing this. Many prewar proponents and practitioners of the modern style had been Jewish, and survivors of the Holocaust settled in Israel and revived their careers.

Before the State

Among the first synagogues built under the British Mandate, perhaps the most important from the standpoint of design and politics was the Great Synagogue in Tel Aviv, built in 1930 in a monumental style that combines

Opposite: The Rabbi Isaac Aboad Synagogue in Safed, Israel, is one of six old synagogues in the city famed for its scholars and mystics. Until the creation of the state of Israel in 1948, synagogues in Safed and Jerusalem were the only centers of religious Judaism in the Holy Land. *Above:* While most pre-twentieth-century Jews in what is now Israel were Sephardic, early immigrants from Eastern Europe settled in the holy city of Safed, where they built the Ha-ari (Rabbi Ari) Synagogue at the end of the sixteenth century. After an earthquake in 1837, the synagogue was rebuilt with an elaborately decorated Polish-style ark.

traditional elements such as arched windows and a large central dome with the plain, smooth wall surfaces and combined massing of blocklike forms typical in early European modernism. The building is similar to the synagogue of Zilina, Slovakia, designed by the early modernist Peter Behrens.

The Yeshurun Synagogue on King George Avenue in Jerusalem, designed by A. Friedmann, M. Rubin, and E. Stolzer, and built in 1934-35, adopted a more radical modernist style, eschewing the complex hierarchical arrangement of multiple forms for a large and simple structure joining only two main masses: a rectangular block, entered on its long side, with a tall half cylinder, housing the sanctuary, joined to the rear.

The Great Synagogue

More recently, the Great Synagogue in Jerusalem, which opened in 1982, continues the modernist vocabulary of the 1930s, albeit in a somewhat updated form. The main sanctuary is hexagonal, recalling the shape of the Star of David. Unlike most Israeli synagogues, it incorporates some stained-glass decoration in five tall, narrow windows over the ark. (Jerusalem's Hadassah Hospital Synagogue, designed by Joseph Neufeld, also has stained glass–the much-admired lantern windows designed by artist Marc Chagall, representing the twelve tribes of Israel.) Like most other buildings in the city, the Great Synagogue is built of the warm yellow limestone mined locally.

Above: THE GREAT SYNAGOGUE IN JERUSALEM, DEDICATED IN 1982, MIXES TRADITIONAL FORMS AND MATERIALS, SUCH AS THE DOME AND JERUSALEM LIMESTONE, IN AN OTHERWISE STARKLY MODERN DESIGN. *Opposite:* THE ISRAEL GOLDSTEIN SYNAGOGUE, DESIGNED BY HEINZ RAU AND DAVID REZNIK, ON THE GIVAT RAM CAMPUS OF HEBREW UNIVERSITY, USES CONCRETE AND GLASS TO CREATE AN ORGANIC DESIGN THAT APPEARS TO HAVE JUST SPROUTED FROM THE GROUND OR LANDED FROM ABOVE.

Experiments with Modern Materials

For various reasons—tradition, climate, light, security—Israeli synagogues tend to be built of stone or concrete and look massive, whatever their size. A synagogue at Hadera built in 1935 included a watchtower and courtyard to shelter up to two thousand people in case of an attack. While Israeli architects have not adopted the skin of glass favored by many synagogue architects in America in the 1960s and 1970s, they have experimented with concrete to create sculptural forms.

The synagogue in Beersheba, built in 1961 and used by an Ashkenazi-Sephardi congregation, nestles under a sweeping concrete vault that covers the sanctuary like a turtle shell. The vault is anchored in the ground to either side of the small prayer hall, which is lit by a wall perforated from floor to ceiling by hexagonal openings.

Unlike the Beersheba synagogue, which is so rooted to the earth, the Israel Goldstein Synagogue—designed by Heinz Rau and David Reznik and dedicated in 1957—on the Givat Ram campus of the Hebrew University appears ready to float away. This windowless synagogue looks almost like a giant balloon; its smooth, white bulbous form seems to levitate off the ground, at which level it is pierced with wide arched openings that light the entire structure, including the sanctuary encased in the building's upper part.

In Tel Aviv, the Hechal Yehuda Synagogue, built in 1980, is constructed of concrete molded to look like a giant shell—an appropriate form for its seaside location.

POSTWAR EUROPEAN SYNAGOGUES

WHILE MOST POSTWAR European synagogues were modest in size and scale and made little effort to assert their presence within the cityscape, a few communities took bold steps to produce synagogues that could not be ignored. The most dramatic of these is the new synagogue of Livorno, Italy, dedicated in 1962 to replace the destroyed Sephardic synagogue.

On the outside, the new expressive structure is defined by a series of crooked concrete but-

tresses, which, connected by concrete walls, exert intense pressure to hold the building together, allowing a large unimpeded interior sanctuary. Like its Renaissance predecessor, this synagogue has seats all around, in this case forming a horseshoe plan around the projecting central bimah. The women's gallery has a transparent parapet wall, more open than the gilded-metal grilles of the old synagogue that it replaces.

Also of note is the Ruhrallee Synagogue at Essen, Germany, built in 1959 and designed by Dieter Knoblauch and Heinz Heise, situated on the site of Erich Mendolsohn's Jewish Youth

Center (1931). Like Mendolsohn's design for Park Synagogue in Cleveland, Ohio, the primary element in Essen is a hemisphere that rises directly from the ground—there is visible substructure, but no drum. The simple unified shape may symbolize the monotheism of Judaism but it also reflects contemporary trends in architecture, specifically a search for pure geometric forms. Inside, there are more simple shapes. The ark is a rectangle inscribed within a broad triangle. At the apex of the dome, a Star of David set within a circle is inscribed, articulated with a series of small round windows, which define the shape with light.

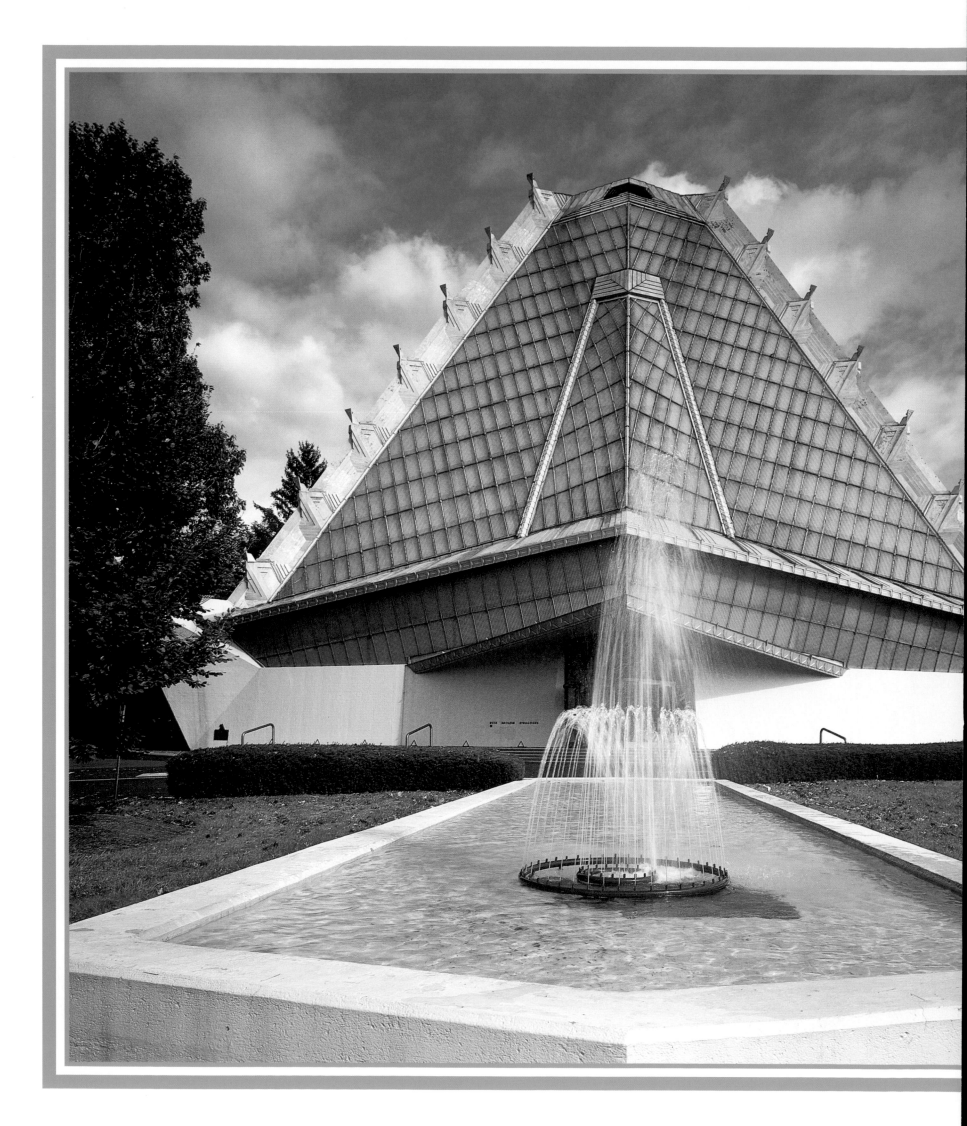

FREEDOM

Synagogues in North America

❧

JEWS LEFT EUROPE FOR THE NEW WORLD, particularly the United States, in three main waves. In the sixteenth and seventeenth centuries, Spanish Jews and their descendants settled in many New World and Asian ports along the developing trade routes. A small but prosperous Sephardic Jewish population lived in the United States and participated in the War of Independence. These Jews built synagogues in Philadelphia, New York, Newport, Charleston, and Savannah before the end of the eighteenth century.

Pages 100-101: Frank Lloyd Wright created a multifaceted mountain of light for Beth Sholom Congregation in Elkins Park, Pennsylvania. Using new materials, including a range of plastics and resins, Wright built a structure that looks solid outside but shimmers with colored light within. *Page 101, detail:* A stained glass window in Jonesboro, Mississippi. *Above and opposite:* Newport, Rhode Island's Touro Synagogue, designed by noted colonial-period architect Peter Harrison, is the oldest surviving synagogue in the United States, though its Georgian exterior gives no hint of its Jewish function. The soothing proportions and soft details inside are elegant examples of fine Georgian architecture.

In the mid-nineteenth century, thousands of central European Jews joined the mass immigration to the United States caused by political unrest and economic instability in Europe. Despite improvements in post-Emancipation Europe, Jews from Germany, France, Bohemia, and elsewhere sought a better life in North America. Many eventually abandoned Judaism, but others formed small communities, built synagogues, and continued traditions.

From the 1880s to the 1920s hundreds of thousands of "Russian" Jews settled in North America and South America as well as Australia. This wave of emigration from Europe was by far the biggest. Millions of Jews fled eastern Europe, particularly those territories controlled by Russia and repressed under Tsarist rule. Many others did not move so far, migrating to Germany, France, Great Britain, and even Ireland. In the British Isles, the new arrivals upset and overwhelmed the existing older community, much of it Sephardic.

In the United States, the immigrants numerically overwhelmed the older Sephardic and German populations, though it took over a generation before they established political and economic dominance.

AMERICAN STYLES

AMERICAN SYNAGOGUE architecture has mostly followed the general design and building trends of American religious architecture, though on several occasions influences from European synagogues have been felt.

The first Jewish communities accepted contemporary American styles, as can be seen in the Georgian classicism of Peter Harrison's Touro Synagogue in Newport, Rhode Island (1753); the Greek Revival Shearith Israel in New York City (1834, demolished); Beth Elohim

in Charleston, South Carolina (1841); and Baltimore Hebrew Congregation in Baltimore, Maryland (1845). Jews even went along with experiments in Egyptian Revival in keeping with the fashion of the time; Mikveh Israel Synagogue of Philadelphia (1824–25) designed by William Strickland, and the same city's Crown Street synagogue designed by Thomas U. Walter (1849, demolished) were in this style. It is curious, but not surprising, given regular communication in the Jewish (and English-speaking) world, that communities as distant as those in America and in Australia chose similar designs.

The Moorish style, inspired by developments in central Europe in the 1840s, was adopted in the United States by many groups of first-generation German Jews, who had arrived in large numbers in the 1840s but were not prosperous enough to build large synagogues until after the American Civil War. Examples include the Plum Street Synagogue in Cincinnati, Ohio (1866); Central Synagogue, New York City (1872); Oheb Shalom, Newark, New Jersey (1884); Eldridge St. Synagogue, New York City (1886); and the tiny Gemilleth Chassid in Port Gibson, Mississippi (1891) can still be seen, but most of the opulent synagogues have been demolished, replaced by more subdued, often classical structures.

By the late nineteenth century increasingly assimilated Jews found the Moorish style too

Left: THE ARCHITECTURE OF MANY AMERICAN SYNA-GOGUES BUILT IN THE NINETEENTH CENTURY WAS INSPIRED BY CHURCHES. IN NO PLACE IS THIS MORE EVIDENT THAN SAVANNAH, GEORGIA, WHERE TEMPLE MIKVAH ISRAEL WAS BUILT IN 1876 IN A HIGH GOTHIC STYLE, WITH A TALL CENTRAL TOWER. *Opposite:* TEMPLE EMANU-EL IN NEW YORK CITY, COMPLETED IN 1929, IS THE CULMINATION OF ROMANESQUE STYLE IN SYNAGOGUE ARCHITECTURE. THE ENORMOUS FIFTH AVENUE FACADE ARCH IS ECHOED AT THE END OF A LONG NAVE BY AN ARCH OF SIMILAR SIZE OVER THE ARK.

exotic and un-American. New classical edifices—dignified, austere, monumental, and reflective of the favored style of America's cultural elite—were built. In 1897 Arnold Brunner designed a new home for Shearith Israel in New York City, followed by Temple Society of Concord in Syracuse, New York, in 1910. While overtly responding to general architectural trends fostered by the Columbian Exposition of 1893, Brunner justified his use of the classical style by citing discoveries in Palestine of ancient synagogues—all classical buildings.

The spirit of integration lay behind the more classical structures of Congregation Beth El, Detroit (1903); Beth Ahabah, Richmond (1904); the Sephardic Mikveh Israel, Philadelphia (1909, demolished); and Anshe Sholom (1910, demolished) and Sinai Temple (1909-12, demolished) in Chicago.

The Byzantine-Revival style was common for synagogues at the beginning of the twentieth century and became particularly popular after World War I. The central dome over the sanctuary space became especially popular. A common urban variation of this style emphasized a single, giant facade portal, as at B'nai Jeshurun, New York (1918), and Temple Emanu-El (1929), also in New York.

Top, left: THE SMALL TIPHERETH ISRAEL SYNAGOGUE, BUILT IN 1889 IN ALLIANCE, NEW JERSEY, SERVED THE JEWISH AGRICULTURAL COMMUNITY FOUNDED THERE IN THE 1880S. IT LOOKS VERY MUCH LIKE THE WOOD-FRAME AND CLAPBOARD HOUSES OF THE CONGREGATION MEMBERS, BUT THE EAST WALL HAS TWO TALL WINDOWS BETWEEN WHICH THE ARK IS SET BELOW A SMALL ROUND WINDOW. *Bottom, left:* ARCHITECT JOHN W.H. WATTS DESIGNED OTTAWA'S ADATH JESHURUN SYNAGOGUE IN 1904, BASING THE CANADIAN SYNAGOGUE ON CENTRAL EUROPEAN EXAMPLES. THE TWO-TOWERED FACADE IS TYPICAL OF NORTH AMERICAN SYNAGOGUES OF THE PERIOD. *Opposite:* MOORISH ELEMENTS WERE ALSO USED IN THE TEMPLE OF ISRAEL BUILT IN WILMINGTON, NORTH CAROLINA, IN 1875-76. HERE, THE FACADE FLANKED BY DOMED TOWERS IS INDEBTED TO RECENT SYNAGOGUES IN THE CITIES OF BERLIN, BUDAPEST, AND NEW YORK.

Australia: The Other New World

In Australia, Jews from eastern Europe represented the first significant settlement of Jews in that country, though as early as 1831 Jews from England had established a congregation in Sydney and built their first synagogue, a small Egyptian Revival structure on York Street, in 1844.

Similar synagogues were constructed in Hobart, Tasmania, in 1845 and in Adelaide in 1850. More Jews came the the area during the gold rush of the 1850s. The cathedral-like Great Synagogue of Sydney, consecrated in 1878 and built in a Gothic-influenced eclectic style, was used to elevate the visibility and social status of Australian Jews.

Opposite: KHAL ADATH JESHURUN, BETTER KNOWN AS THE ELDRIDGE ST. SYNAGOGUE, WAS THE FIRST GRAND SYNAGOGUE ERECTED BY EASTERN EUROPEAN IMMIGRANTS IN THE UNITED STATES. THE FACADE, WHICH DOMINATES THE NARROW STREET, COMBINES ROMANESQUE AND MOORISH ELEMENTS. *Right:* THE FACADE AND TOWERS OF NEW YORK CITY'S CENTRAL SYNAGOGUE, WHICH WAS DESIGNED BY HENRY FERNBACH IN 1872, ARE MODELED ON THE DOHANY STREET SYNAGOGUE OF BUDAPEST. THE SYNAGOGUE WAS SERIOUSLY DAMAGED BY A FIRE IN 1998 BUT IS BEING RESTORED.

THE MODERN SYNAGOGUE

JEWISH COMMUNITIES were quicker to embrace Art Deco and other variants of modernism than were other religious communities, but few synagogues were built in the 1930s. However, immediately after World War II, the demand for new synagogues in the suburbs created a building boom of modern-style synagogues in the late 1940s and 1950s.

Left and below: DOMED SYNAGOGUES BECAME EXTREMELY POPULAR IN THE 1920S AND 1930S. MANY SYNAGOGUES ADAPTED BYZANTINE MASSING AND DECORATIVE MOTIFS INTO A MORE STREAMLINED ART DECO STYLE, AS AT TEMPLE EMANUEL IN PATTERSON, NEW JERSEY, DESIGNED BY FREDERIC WENTWORTH, AND AT THE WATERBURY, CONNECTICUT, SYNAGOGUE DESIGNED BY NATHAN MYERS. BOTH SYNAGOGUES OPENED IN 1929.

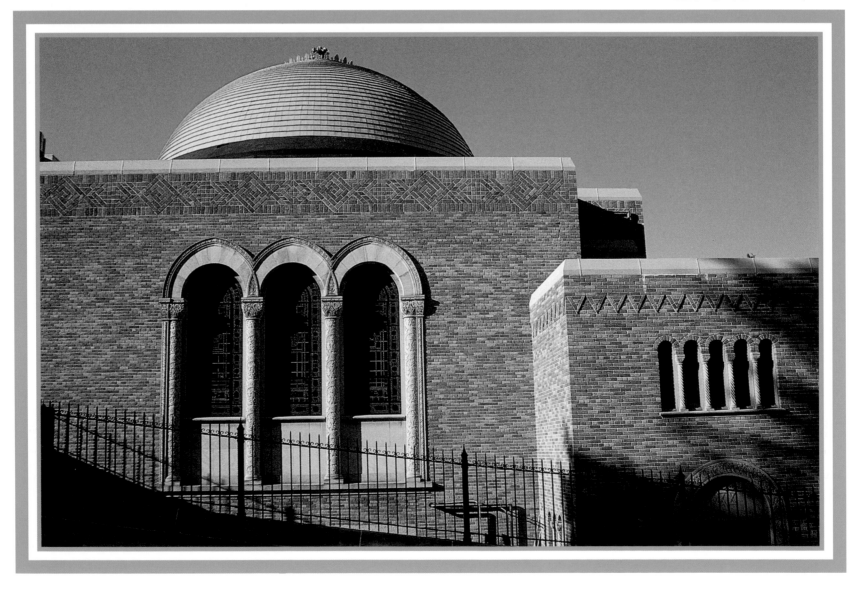

Temple Beth El built circa 1913 in Helena, Arkansas, is typical of scores of synagogues erected across the United States between 1893, when the Classical style became popular thanks to the Columbian exposition in Chicago, and the start of World War I. Jews were still trying to find a style for synagogues that would make them distinct from Christian architecture, and Classicism offered an alternative to the exotic Moorish Revival. Moreover, archaeological finds of ancient synagogues in Palestine allowed the argument that the earliest synagogues were Classical buildings, too.

Erich Mendolsohn

In America, postwar synagogue design was transformed by the exciting work of Erich Mendolsohn, the German Jewish expressionist refugee who established a second and extremely productive career in the United States.

After a stint in Palestine, where he built various hospital and university buildings, Mendolsohn designed his first synagogue in America, completed in 1950, for Congregation B'nai Amoona in St. Louis, Missouri, where he developed two important concepts for modern synagogue design. The first was primarily expressive and symbolic—the accentuation of the sanctuary section of a large complex using elevated and curvilinear forms. At B'nai Amoona this took the form of a dramatic parabolic roof that rises from the ark wall to the entrance wall, the top of which is glazed, allowing light to pour over the congregation and onto the bimah and ark.

At the Park Synagogue in Cleveland, Ohio, Mendolsohn designed a hemispheric dome, 100 feet (30m) in diameter, which rests on a drum made of ten supports that alternate with large plate-glass windows. Because of the low drum, however, and the overall horizontal definition of the complex, the sanctuary dome appears to rise straight from the ground. The

dome sits at the point of a dramatic triangular plan, nestled into a wooded area overlooking Cleveland Heights.

Mendolsohn also created adaptable spaces that could be connected or separated by sliding partitions and could be arranged to serve diverse functions at different times of the day or year. This was particularly important to American congregations, which often had large memberships but small attendance for all but High Holiday services. Such design allowed the construction of smaller, more intimate sanctuaries to be used for daily and weekly services, and

permitted the expansion of these spaces to accommodate the overflow crowds on Rosh Hashanah and Yom Kippur.

The expansion of synagogues to include additional spaces was increasingly required as new communities relocated and recreated the diverse offerings of older Jewish neighborhoods in new, essentially artificial environments. Mendolsohn's designs in this regard, which were quickly understood and adapted by the prolific synagogue architect Percival Goodman, formed the basis of most suburban synagogue architecture from the late 1940s through the 1980s.

Percival Goodman

Percival Goodman built more than fifty synagogues in his lifetime. His creations are more austere than those of Mendolsohn but his designs are generally comfortable and highly functional.

Goodman preferred smaller, lower rectangular units arranged in artful, but primarily practical, ways. In this, he utilized Mendolsohn's development of adaptable space. But rather than use a sculptural language in architecture Goodman more often incorporated modern sculpture and other art techniques

Opposite: Temple Ohabai Shalom in Brookline, Massachusetts, built in 1928, is a fine example of a Byzantine-style synagogue. Its broad dome is modeled on Hagia Sophia in Istanbul; the original design included a large corner tower that resembled a Turkish minaret. *Above:* Percival Goodman designed Temple Beth Emeth in Albany, New York, dedicated in 1957. As in all of his many designs, Goodman worked closely with artists—in this case Robert Sowers, who designed the seven stained glass windows visible here, which stand like an abstract menorah behind the wooden ark carved by Nathaniel Kaz. The roof suggestive of a tent is typical of Goodman's work.

into his work to accent elements. This was first done at his 1951 B'nai Israel in Millburn, New Jersey, where he installed a large abstract sculpture, *Burning Bush* by Herbert Ferber, on the exterior, set on a wedge-shaped cypress-paneled protrusion, which supports the artwork and also extends the ark itself—set within the inner wall—outside the building line. The ark protrusion and sculpture are flanked by two large windows that make up the rest of the ark wall. These are divided into smaller panels in an abstract design, recalling the geometry of Piet Mondrian's paintings. In the center of the north window is set a large Star of David.

At Goodman's Temple Beth El in Springfield, Massachusetts, a 19-foot-high (5.8m) abstract bronze *Pillar of Fire* by Ibram Lassaw was installed on the exterior of the ark wall. The sculpture is the only ornament in sight; the supporting walls have been left plain and blank. Goodman's integration of modern sculpture into synagogue design became a featured style of postwar American synagogues. In many instances, the architecture serves as an almost neutral background or frame.

Goodman continued to experiment in synagogue design from the 1950s through the 1970s. Like Mendolsohn, he worked hard to utilize natural light for dramatic effect in his buildings. He employed several methods for this, including the frequent introduction of patterned stained-glass windows to alter the intensity and color of light; he also used the placement of irregularly shaped windows— long and tall, or small and squat—in key places opposite elements he wished to emphasize so that he could expect dramatic shafts of light to appear at certain times of the day and have more diffuse lighting at other times.

Most of all, however, like most of his contemporaries, Goodman allowed plenty of light in, hoping to create airy, welcoming spaces.

Frank Lloyd Wright and Beth Sholom Congregation

One of the best-known modern synagogues was designed by Frank Lloyd Wright for Beth Sholom Congregation in Elkins Park, Pennsylvania.

The building, which owes much to earlier synagogue design, was completed in 1959. To

some extent, Wright took the ideas fashioned by Mendolsohn—a high vaulted space for the sanctuary, visible from afar, and embracing within—in a new direction. Rather than an expressive, but soft and caressing, curved vault, Wright designed an angular, almost crystalline form to create a "mountain of light." Covered with tinted glass and plastics, the building can appear translucent on a bright day. When lit from within at night, the struc-

ture glows. The singularity of the building is enhanced by its standing free from ancillary structures; thus Wright's glass mountain gains monumentality by standing alone, creating an explicit image of Mt. Sinai.

Wright's design, though never copied, was immediately influential, and other architects set out to top his imagery, creating a series of dramatic sculpted forms. Shortly after the completion of Beth Sholom, Percival Goodman designed the most striking of his synagogues. His 1963 Shaarey Zedek in Southfield, Michigan, features a main sanctuary covered with a tremendously high pitched roof, reaching a jagged pinnacle over the ark. The interior tent-like effect of the design recalls the biblical instructions for the erection of the Tabernacle, but the jagged concrete exterior profile evokes the rugged geology of Mt. Sinai and immediately calls Wright's synagogue to mind.

Around the same time, architect Sidney Eisenstadt built in El Paso, Texas, the Mount Sinai Temple, which introduced the tent/tower element into a desert setting with an arched concrete shell that seems to grow organically from its site. The design is simple and stark. Unlike Wright, Eisenstadt linked his design to the actual topography, letting the congregants see the profiles of distant mountains through an arched window above the ark.

Sculptural Forms

In the 1960s, when almost all synagogues built were freestanding, and frequently placed in a landscaped setting, the trend toward creating sculptural forms, often with the use of pliant concrete vaults, increased. These have been popularly likened to flying saucers; they are often circular in plan, bulbous in profile, and austere. Like Mendolsohn's Cleveland dome, there are few windows piercing their vaults, which may extend all the way to the ground.

Two distinctive variants on this type, designed by Minoru Yamasaki, the architect best known for the World Trade Center Towers in New York, are Congregation Israel in Glencoe, Illinois (1964), and Temple Beth El in Detroit, Michigan. The Glencoe Synagogue is noted for its structural innovation—a number of large concrete arches that frame the building and bend

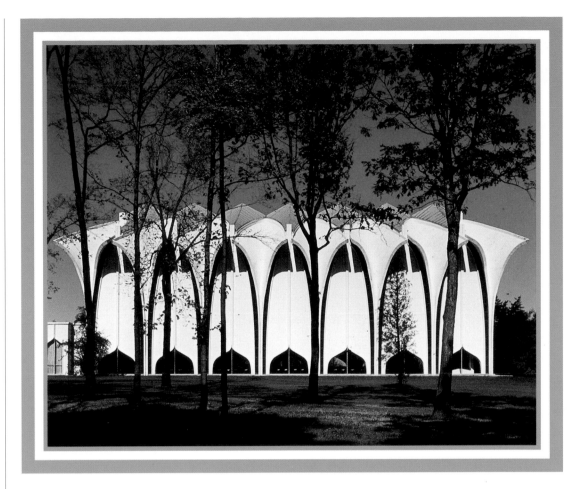

Opposite: FRANK LLOYD WRIGHT EXPRESSED HIS INTENT FOR THE INTERIOR OF CONGREGATION BETH SHOLOM, SAYING: "WE WANT TO CREATE THE KIND OF BUILDING THAT PEOPLE, ON ENTERING IT, WILL FEEL AS IF THEY WERE RESTING IN THE VERY HANDS OF GOD." *Above:* CONGREGATION ISRAEL IN GLENCOE, ILLINOIS, DESIGNED BY MINORU YAMASAKI, IS EVERY BIT AS INNOVATIVE IN DESIGN AND MATERIALS AS WRIGHT'S BETH SHOLOM. A SERIES OF LARGE CONCRETE ARCHES FRAMES THE BUILDING, BUT LARGE GAPS IN THE STRUCTURE FILL THE SANCTUARY WITH FILTERED LIGHT.

inward to meet at the center of the long sanctuary. Outside, the appearance is disconcerting. On ground level a series of delicate Gothic arches are punched into the larger arched segments. Above, the segments bulge and bend like the shell of a concrete crustacean. The white building changes shape from every direction. Inside, the pendentives between the big framing arches become flat openings in a tentlike ceiling. They are glazed, allowing light to flood the interior. The tall, thin, gilded teak ark, which has been described as embracing the Torah scrolls like a prayer shawl, is the focus of the long vista as glimpsed from the sanctuary entrance.

Other leading American modernists such as Walter Gropius and Philip Johnson have

designed synagogues, as well. Gropius's 1960 Temple Oheb Shalom in Baltimore is a muscular design accented on each flank by four tall arched bays, which continue as barrel vaults through the structure. Johnson, for the 1964 Kneses Tifereth Israel Synagogue in Port Chester, New York, created a sleek, perforated, white rectangle preceded by a mausoleumlike oval vestibule with a saucer dome. The main box is a steel frame, and supports remain visible on the exterior, dividing the structure into seven bays. These are filled with large stone slabs interspersed with narrow windows. It has been described as an enormous jewel box, perhaps because of the soft light that passes through the many colored windows.

THE RETURN OF HISTORY

In the early 1960s, elements of historicism began to appear in modern synagogue design. Particularly after the publication in English of *Wooden Synagogues* (1959), by Kazimierz and Maria Piechotka, interest grew in the lost wooden synagogues of Poland. Modern architects, such as Louis Kahn and Davis,

Brody & Wisniewski sought to incorporate recollections of Poland's lost Jewish legacy in their contemporary designs.

Davis, Brody & Wisniewski's 1963 synagogue in Lakewood, New Jersey, did this best. It features a high central sanctuary wrapped in a low annex ring, part of which serves as a library, all on an octagonal plan. Like its Polish ancestors (and unlike most contemporary synagogues), this shul has a central bimah. In elevation,

Davis, Brody & Wisniewski designed a high double roof, which recalls the multiform pitched roofs of Poland. The building was originally intended to be constructed entirely of wood, but the exterior was changed to concrete and steel to meet insurance requirements.

Louis Kahn also designed a small synagogue based on eastern European models. The 1972 Reform Temple Beth El in Chappaqua, New York, is a two-story octagonal wood and concrete structure surmounted by a 30-foot (9m) clerestory version of a Polish hipped and gabled roof. The interior, with its central bimah, was lit by a skylight of wood-framed glass panels, and the walls are paneled with warm wood. At the synagogue dedication Kahn said, "What we have done in this very, very understated place has glory in it. I feel the great continuum here."

Other elements of the Polish synagogues are coming into fashion, notably wood itself. After several decades of building in brick and concrete or steel and glass, synagogue architects have begun to turn to natural materials. Part of this stems from an awareness of the legacy of wooden synagogues, and part to a more general shift in architectural preference for warmer, more intimate spaces and finishes. Both these interests come together in a group of small structures that represent the best in a new synagogue design.

Two recent synagogues exemplify the trend. The 1989 Gates of Grove Synagogue in East Hampton, Long Island, by Norman Jaffe, marries the local seaside vernacular, with weathered shingles and gabled roofs, to the Polish wood tradition. The building is designed with sleek modern lines, but the abundance of wood and light, the repeated use of elements in groups of ten (as in the ten attributes of God), and the ascending ranks of archlike forms in the sanctuary, all recall, in spirit, the eastern European past of the congregants. Like much of modern Judaism, the synagogue displays a search for roots, but betrays no intention of relinquishing contemporary style and relevance. Similarly, the 1996 Temple Israel in Greenfield, Massachusetts, by architect M. Louis Goodman, integrates local and traditional forms utilizing natural materials. Its design recalls Poland and the Ukraine as well as local New England prototypes.

In buildings like these, the modern synagogue has joined with the past.

Opposite: THE INTERIOR OF CONGREGATION ISRAEL IN GLENCOE, ILLINOIS, IS SPACIOUS, AND THE USE OF LIGHT, THE WHITE WALLS, AND LITTLE ORNAMENTATION CREATE A CEREBRAL SPACE. THE TALL THIN GILDED ARK HAS BEEN LIKENED TO A PRAYER SHAWL WRAPPING THE TORAH SCROLLS, BUT FROM THE SANCTUARY ENTRANCE IT ALSO SUGGESTS A SINGLE FLAME—A BURNING BUSH OR ETERNAL LIGHT. *Above:* ARCHITECT LOUIS KAHN'S TEMPLE BETH EL IN CHAPPAQUA, NEW YORK, IS PERHAPS HIS MOST INTIMATELY SCALED SPACE. AS IN HIS OTHER WORK, KAHN MIXES PURE GEOMETRIC SHAPES AND VOLUMES WITH WARM MATERIALS AND FINISHES.

GLOSSARY

Aedicule: An architectural framing motif formed by two columns supporting an entablature and pediment. Frequently used for doorways and windows, and in synagogues for the ark.

Apse: A semicircular or polygonal end of a synagogue, church, or other basilica, which usually projects from the rectangular plan of the main building space.

Ark (Hebrew: Aron ha-Kodesh): Usually a cabinet for keeping Torah scrolls, but can also be a small adjacent room. The ark is almost always situated against the synagogue wall closest to Jerusalem. It is the focal point of the synagogue and is usually highly decorated.

Ashkenazic (Ashkenazi): Derived from the term Ashkenaz, a medieval Hebrew term for Germany, it signifies the Jewish cultural and religious milieu including western, central, and eastern Europe.

Basilica: In ancient Rome, an oblong building used as a hall of justice; in the early Christian era, a church built on the plan of such a hall. Most basilicas are rectangular in plan with more than one aisle.

Bet haKnesset: Literal translation from Hebrew is house of gathering/assembly; synagogue.

Bet haMidrash: Literal translation from Hebrew is house of study; may also refer to a synagogue. (See **Study house**.)

Bimah: Platform and table in a synagogue from which the Torah scrolls are read.

Chair of Elijah: A special chair in the vicinity of the ark set aside for the Prophet Elijah during circumcision ceremonies.

Decalogue (Tablets of the Law): An artistic representation of the stone tablets on which were inscribed the Ten Commandments given by God to Moses on Mount Sinai.

Esnoga: Sephardic term for synagogue.

Eternal light (Hebrew: ner tamid): A continuously burning lamp that hangs in front of the Aron ha-Kodesh, meant to remind viewers of the omnipresence of God.

Etrog: Citrus fruit used with the lulav to celebrate the holiday of Sukkot.

Gallery: An open upper story above an aisle of the nave.

Hassid (also Chassid): Member of a Jewish mystic sect founded in eastern Europe in the eighteenth century and characterized by joyous, sometimes frenzied, worship and strict observance.

Hechal: Preferred Sephardic term for the ark.

Kristallnacht: The night and day of November 9–10, 1938, when Nazi-inspired gangs looted Jewish property throughout Germany and Austria and destroyed hundreds of synagogues.

Lulav: Palm frond entwined with springs of myrtle and willow, used with the etrog to celebrate the holiday of Sukkot.

Magen David: Star of David.

Mechitzah: Divider separating the men's and women's sections of a synagogue.

Menorah (pl: menorot): A seven-branched candelabrum found in the biblical sanctuary and Jerusalem Temple; a similar candelabrum found in a synagogue; an eight-branched candelabrum used during the Hanukkah festival.

Mikvah (pl: mikvot): Ritual bath facility employing fresh-flowing water, used for monthly cleansing rituals for women and analogous rituals for men.

Minyan: Ten adults (sometimes ten men) required for the reciting of certain prayers.

Moorish: Architectural style developed in the mid-nineteenth century incorporating elements from the architecture and decoration of Muslim Spain and other exotic locales. Typical elements include horseshoe arches, arabesques, and minaretlike towers.

Nave: The central aisle of a basilica—in a synagogue, usually where the primary worship space is located. In Orthodox synagogues the bimah is often placed in the nave.

Ner tamid: See **Eternal light**.

Orthodox: Jewish practice strictly adhering to age-old traditions as codified by sixteenth-century writers Joseph Caro and Moses Isserles.

Parochet: Curtain in front of the ark in a synagogue.

Pier: A solid masonry support, similar to a column, but rectangular.

Reform Judaism: A movement that emerged in the early nineteenth-century aimed to modernize Jewish practice to fit the conditions of contemporary life.

Sephardic (Sephardi): Referring to Jewish traditions originating in Spain and spreading throughout the world after the expulsion of the Jews from that country in 1492.

Siddur: Jewish prayer book.

Study house: School and religious discussion room. May be annexed to a synagogue or separately built. It may have an ark and a bimah so that people can use it for prayer.

Talmud: Record of legal decisions and discussions of ancient Jewish sages—the fundamental work of the Oral Law that complements the Written Law (Pentateuch).

Tevah: Sephardic term for bimah.

Tik (also tiq): Near Eastern wood or metal case for the Torah scroll.

Torah: Written Law; the Pentateuch. Handwritten on parchment scrolls, it is kept in the synagogue ark.

Vault: An arched structure often forming a ceiling or roof.

BIBLIOGRAPHY

Barnavi, Eli (ed.). *Historical Atlas of the Jewish People.* New York: Knopf, 1992.

de Breffny, Brian. *The Synagogue.* New York: Macmillan, 1978.

Encyclopaedia Judaica, 1971–72. Jerusalem: Encyclopaedia Judaica, 1973.

Fine, Steven (ed.). *Sacred Realm: The Emergence of the Synagogue in the Ancient Realm.* New York: Yeshiva University Museum/Oxford University Press, 1996.

Greenberg, Evelyn. "Sanctity in the Woodwork," *Hadassah* Magazine (October 1996), 29–32.

Grossman, Grace Cohen. *Jewish Art.* Southport, CT.: Hugh Lauter Levin Assoc., 1995.

Kampf, Avram. *Contemporary Synagogue Art: Developments in the United States, 1945–1965.* Philadelphia: Jewish Publication Society of America, 1966.

Krinsky, Carol Herselle. *The Synagogues of Europe: Architecture, History, Meaning.* New York and Cambridge, MA.: Architectural History Foundation/MIT Press, 1985 (reprint, 1996; Dover Publications).

Levine, Lee I. (ed.). *Ancient Synagogues Revealed.* Jerusalem and Detroit: Israel Exploration Society/Wayne State University Press, 1982.

Piechotka, Maria and Kazimierz. *Wooden Synagogues.* Warsaw: Arkady, 1959.

Recent American Synagogue Architecture (exh. cat.). New York: Jewish Theological Seminary of America/Jewish Museum, 1963.

Urman, Dan, and Paul V.M. Flesher (eds.). *Ancient Synagogues: Historical Analysis and Archaeological Discovery.* 2 vols. Leiden and New York: E.J. Brill, 1995.

Wigoder, Geoffrey. *The Story of the Synagogue.* Jerusalem: Domino Press, 1986.

Wischnitzer, Rachel. *Synagogue Architecture in the United States: History and Interpretation.* Philadelphia: Jewish Publication Society of America, 1955.

—————————. *The Architecture of the European Synagogue.* Philadelphia: Jewish Publication Society of America, 1964.

Zack, Joel. *The Synagogues of Morocco: An Architectural and Preservation Survey.* New York: World Monuments Fund, 1993.

INDEX